WHEN WE'RE IN CHARGE

Praise for WHEN WE'RE IN CHARGE by Amanda Litman

"Enough already with the quiet quitting: Amanda Litman understands that the world is better when we get involved, lead with principle, and don't give up. *When We're in Charge* is the new essential handbook for taking power and actually using it to do good." —**Jon Favreau, Jon Lovett, And Tommy Vietor, Crooked Media Reads**

"A refreshingly candid, delightfully irreverent guide to leadership for the next generation. Amanda Litman busts some major myths about how to succeed at the helm. Get ready to rethink some of your basic assumptions about authenticity, productivity, and professionalism." —**Adam Grant, #1 *New York Times* bestselling author of *Hidden Potential* and *Think Again*, and host of the podcast *Re:Thinking***

"This is essential reading for any Gen Z or millennial who holds a leadership position or one day hopes to. The next generation of leadership is primed to look and act like nothing that's come before, and Amanda Litman has given them the road map to do exactly that." —**Jason Kander, *New York Times* bestselling author of *Invisible Storm* and *Outside the Wire*, and first millennial elected to statewide office**

"*When We're in Charge* will help you be the boss you wished you had. This book is chock full of information and guidance—anyone under 40 will come away with invaluable insights into the changing workplace and how they can successfully lead their teams with compassion (and still get sh*t done.)" —**Tori Dunlap, *New York Times* bestselling author of *Financial Feminist* and founder of Her First $100k**

"The workplace is evolving more rapidly than ever. *When We're in Charge* has all the insights and advice for leaders to navigate these choppy waters." —**Sami Sage, *New York Times* bestselling author of *Democracy in Retrograde***

"*When We're in Charge* continues Amanda Litman's legacy of mapping out systems for millennials & Gen Z, who believe in basic human rights for all Americans, to take ownership of our institutions and make this country one we're proud to be living in, as a generation. She is a leader I turn to in times of democratic despair, and this book makes the practice of leadership clear, direct, and accessible." **—Ilana Glazer**

"With *When We're in Charge,* Amanda Litman does the impossible: she provides clear-eyed, actionable advice on how to do meaningful leadership work in fields we're passionate about . . . and *actually keep doing it*. She understands that for Gen Z and millennial workers, *caring* has never been the problem. Figuring out how to *keep* caring—and lead others as they navigate their own careers—is just as important as the work itself. This book is unlike anything else in the 'business book' space—a must-read for anyone who doesn't just want to make the world better, but wants to figure out how 'making the world better' can be one's life's work, not just something we do before burning out in our thirties."
—Anne Helen Petersen, author of *Can't Even* and coauthor of *Out of Office*, and writer of one of the top newsletters, *Culture Study*

"Amanda has written a great leadership book for young people who want to lead like humans and not corporate robots. Millennial managers and leaders face a whole host of challenges that previous generations didn't—we can all be more intentional, thoughtful, empathetic leaders if we ask ourselves the questions Amanda has laid out here. Her personal examples and interviews are a fantastic road map in figuring out what kind of leader you want to be."
—Versha Sharma, editor in chief of *Teen Vogue*

"I think *When We're in Charge*, from my friend Amanda 'Run for Something' Litman, will be this [year's] must-read action and hope manifesto." **—Laura Olin, former social media director for the Obama 2012 Campaign**

WHEN WE'RE IN CHARGE

A PLAYBOOK FOR HOW TO SHOW UP, LEAD WELL, AND GO HOME HAPPY

Amanda Litman

Crooked Media Reads
A zando IMPRINT
NEW YORK

Crooked
Media
Reads

Crooked Media Reads is an imprint of Zando.
zandoprojects.com

Originally published in hardcover by Crooked Media Reads, May 2025.
First trade paperback edition: September 2026

Design by Neuwirth & Associates, Inc.
Cover design by Maura Intemann

Library of Congress Control Number: 2025931230

978-1-63893-192-8 (Hardcover)
978-1-63893-419-6 (Paperback)
978-1-63893-193-5 (ebook)

10 9 8 7 6 5 4 3 2 1
Manufactured in the United States of America
LSCC

For the generation-after-next-gen leaders in my life,
Jo and Franny—and for Declan, who makes it all possible.

CONTENTS

PART THREE

INTRODUCTION

Back in 2017, when I started Run for Something—a political organization that recruits and supports millennials and Gen Zers running for local office—I kept noticing something unusual: At twenty-seven years old, I was regularly the youngest person (and for sure the youngest woman) in many of the rooms I was in.

My role as one of two cofounders was predominantly focused around fundraising and public events, so by necessity, I spent a lot of time with people decades older than me asking for money. I'd put on my "fancy lady" clothes (which, for me, involved a lot of animal print and bright-red lipstick) and try to make the case for investing in the kind of political work that wasn't flashy or exciting but could make a meaningful difference if we did it right.

Meanwhile, my cofounder and I were slowly building a team of employees that were expected to work hard while they were on the job and rest hard when they were off of it. We were tired after years of sprinting from campaign to campaign and wanted our organization's work culture to mirror our mission: long-term and sustainable.

When I first set out to start a company, I was operating without a how-to manual. No one in Democratic politics had successfully built a big organization doing what we were doing before, and in particular, no one had done it while also implementing policies that gave their employees space to be real people outside of work. Nearly every week brought new challenges I hadn't expected.

But I believed (and still believe) in our mission, so I tried to carry myself with the confidence—real or pretend—necessary to get the work done and lead us forward.

Sometime around 2022, something changed. All of a sudden, there were other executives in these rooms who were in the same stage of life as me or even younger, and other organizations who were grappling with the challenges we'd worked through just a year or two before. Many of the leaders we'd helped elect across the country were making national headlines and showing the way millennial and Gen Z politicians could enter spaces not built for us and transform the energy, the focus, and the fire.

Political reporters noticed this trend, too, and a few reached out to ask: What's the common thread among these younger leaders who kept making headlines?

The answer was obvious to me.

Our generations—millennials and Gen Z—lead differently. We have no patience for bullshit—we demand authenticity or, at least, perceived authenticity. We show emotion when it's real, but we're also vigilant about boundaries. We believe that our missions are urgent and important, but we understand that not every task in service of those missions shares that urgency. We've grown up online and understand intuitively how to use the internet strategically.

We believe in inclusivity as both a moral good and as a necessary tactic to achieve our goals. We love our work (sometimes), but few of us want it to be all of who we are. We're collectively trying to break the cycle in nearly every aspect of our lives: to be better bosses, better parents, better leaders than those who came before us.

The more I thought and talked with others about it, the more I realized: This wasn't just true in politics. My TikTok algorithm started showing me parodies about millennial and Gen Z bosses that deeply resonated—little clips that mocked generational divides, with millennial leaders telling their teams, "No, seriously, stop working," with gentle but firm smiles and "Why do I care why you need the PTO? If you need the time, take it!"

There was something simmering under the radar that I could not stop obsessing over: The millennial and Gen Z style of leadership looks different, feels different, and leads to different team cultures. But it felt like no one had put pen to paper on what all of that added up to.

When I looked back at my experience, I realized part of the reason that starting and leading a company was so damn hard is because nearly every example of leadership I had to look to for advice didn't quite fit the moment. The playbooks of the past were only barely useful in advising me on things like how to be myself without giving too much of myself away to my team, or how to post on Instagram if my employees follow me there, or even tactical things like how to actually take family leave as the boss.

If I wanted a new guide on how to lead *now*, I needed to write one myself.

That's what this book is: the advice I wish I'd had over the last nearly ten years, navigating the choppy waters of changing leadership norms, new demands on those in power, and rapidly shifting expectations of what the workplace can and should provide, all in service of a new understanding of what it will look and feel like when we're in charge.

• • •

If I say, "My boss is such a boomer," you almost certainly know what I mean. There's just a certain vibe that comes with boomer leadership—a deep love of institutions; a belief that if they had to struggle, so should we all; a stigmatization of mental health; a refusal to adjust company or team policies to accommodate burnout; and a mistrust of remote work environments because they can't understand how one could build trust through online communications alone.

A boomer boss brags about never taking time off and doesn't understand why you don't want to answer emails on vacation or on weekends. The boomer leader puts no thought into what is posted on their own social media and doesn't know you saw their every comment on some crazy Facebook meme. The boomer leader doesn't see any issues with calling their employees a family. (News flash: If you can fire me, you're not my family!)

The boomer leader has probably been in charge for a while and maybe resents the idea that their continued hold on power is a problem. They are also, unfortunately, facing down the idea of their own mortality—a scary foreshadowing of the inevitable that adds a layer of anxiety into any conversation about change.

The boomer (or Gen Xer, who often lead like the boomers because they have no other examples to look to) leader is everywhere, running nearly everything. Take our government, where in 2025, the average age in the House of Representatives is fifty-eight and the average age in the Senate is sixty-four, and we've certainly elected our last boomer president.[1] In Hollywood, the heads of major studios and streaming services—the ones making key decisions about what kind of TV and movies are green-lighted—are nearly all in their fifties or sixties. The stars of the typical movie or TV show in the late nineties were in their thirties (think: Tom Cruise). Today, the typical movie star is nearing fifty or much older (spoiler: still Tom Cruise).[2]

CEOs are old.[3] Nobel laureates are old. The people running things at the National Institutes of Health are, you guessed it, old. College presidents and tenured faculty—the people leading some of our most forward-looking institutions that specifically serve young people—are also old.[4] Even farmworkers (median age: 56.2), school bus drivers (55.9), and building inspectors (53.2) are older than you might expect.[5] In nearly every industry across the United States, it's boomers or Gen X on top as far as the eye can see.

That's changing in real time. In 2030, the youngest boomer will hit retirement age, and millennials and Gen Z—whom I collectively call next-gen, and a group I'm squarely part of—are projected to make up seventy-four percent of the global workforce. In fact, per Glassdoor surveys in 2025, millennials already make up a majority of all managers and Gen Z make up one in ten of the managerial class.[6] Generational change is not "about to happen"—it's here.

All of us have had our lives directly or indirectly affected by one "big moment in history" after another, whether it was millennials graduating during the 2008 recession, reeling from the 2016 election results, or the COVID pandemic wrecking our formative years. Millennials have been driving a changing relationship to work, to institutions, and to community. And as Gen Z in particular enters the workforce in even greater numbers, they demand more and more out of leaders—more authenticity, more transparency, more politics, more values, more humanity, more community, more power, more everything. All that is compounded by the way AI is rapidly changing how we understand our role in the workforce.

The millennial and Gen Z leaders who are taking power are grappling with those demands—some of which we can satisfy, others we simply can't—while also dealing with the new pressures that generations before us didn't have to bear.

We've been told our entire lives to "be ourselves" and have climbed the career ladder as such, and then hit positions of power and realized: Wow, we actually *really* cannot be ourselves if we're responsible for other people's livelihoods.

We have to think not just about how we show up in "the office"—which, for many of us, is simply Slack and a seemingly unending number of Zoom calls—but also how we show up online, both professionally and personally.

We have been failed by institutions, let down by jobs we love that don't love us back, become disillusioned with the idea of a safety net that never seems to exist when we need it most—and yet, we have to keep showing up.

As of this writing, there is only a small number of millennial and Gen Z executives. (When this book first came out, New York City had not yet elected our first millennial mayor, Zohran Mamdani!) We've had no clear models for how we should show up, so we're making it up as we go, learning from trial and error.

From that trial and error comes this: a no-bullshit guide on how we can and will lead when we're in charge. We'll be *responsibly* authentic. We'll treat all communications—personal and professional—as strategic communications opportunities. We'll create inclusive environments where people can feel safe to be their real selves, but not necessarily their full selves, and we'll be transparent within reason. We'll build community in new ways, never treating our teams like our families or mistaking our employees for our friends, but still being compassionate and humane. And finally, our ambitions will be for more than the big job or fancy corner office—we will want and create space to live full, joyful lives, whatever that means for us.

It's hard as hell. But we're doing it anyway, and as we do, we're redefining everyone's relationships to work, power, and one another.

* * *

One of the great challenges in conversations about leadership, work, or really any self-help-type discourse (which this book arguably falls under) is that ultimately we live in a society.

Consider *Lean In* by Sheryl Sandberg, the urtext of women's leadership, which entirely misses that no amount of leaning in can get over the barriers that American capitalism in particular puts up against women. There are few individual choices that can make up for problems like no universal paid leave, no national childcare policies, no structural fixes for the gender pay gap, etc. It's not that individual choices don't matter—but, rather, every choice is made within the constraints of reality. And alas, reality can feel pretty bleak.

My theory of the case, both for politics specifically and for this book writ large, is simple: Our institutions are made up of people, and the more we can change the people in charge of those institutions, the more we can change those institutions themselves (or proactively decide to tear them down and build new ones). It's slow change, grind-it-out kind of work, often demoralizing, and it will never feel done in our lifetimes.

But imagine if, over the next fifteen years, the four-day workweek became the norm, not the exception, because of the decisions individual leaders collectively made. Imagine what day-to-day life might be like for millions of people if a vast majority of business leaders operated with an eye toward compassion *and* profit, instead of treating those like mutually exclusive options. Picture how much better things might be if your job didn't make you soul-crushingly miserable, even if you don't love it, because at the very least you knew exactly what to expect from your workplace, how to succeed, and what kind of resources it could and could not provide for you.

I sadly don't have solutions for racism, sexism, capitalism, fascism, bigotry, or any other ism that makes moving through the world really fucking hard for so many people. But I do have thoughts (a lot of them, actually) on how, as leaders, we can make things better for those within our spheres of influence while not losing our minds or dignity in the process—and as American society feels darker and harder for so many people, well-run community spaces like work (among others) will be even more important.

As I try to model setting clear expectations, I want to be up-front: This is not a management book or, at least, not exclusively a management book, because management alone is not enough. Management is both a skill and a set of tactics—it's how you break a bigger goal down into actionable projects, delegate out those projects, work with your team to set goals and deadlines, then operate in a constant cycle of feedback and iteration in order to achieve something.

Leadership is about vision—it's seeing the bigger picture in service of the goal, aligning the team around that vision and inspiring them to keep working toward it even when things get hard. There are some things about leadership that may come easier to you depending on your temperament, self-esteem, and resilience (among other traits), but much of leadership is a practice you can refine. Being a good manager can make you a great leader, but you can be a leader without having any direct reports.

What you're about to read is a combination of the two: Some management tips are scattered throughout, but this is intended to be a broader framework of what it means to lead now and into the future. I've broken it down into three parts.

Part one is all about you, inside and out. You've probably been told most of your life to ~just be yourself~. But now that you're a (or *the*) boss, you keep learning the hard way: You absolutely cannot be yourself, at least not fully, and not in the ways pop culture and social media tells us "authenticity" looks like. So now what? How do you be authentic and also in charge? How do you do it in the age of AI, where authenticity is even more important? We'll get into the internal and external work necessary to develop a leadership persona that feels comfortable for you but not sloppy—the self-presentation equivalent of business athleisure, so to speak.

Equally as important, how do you perform that persona? How do you think about what you look like, how you sound, which emojis you use, whether or not you participate in the bullshitting over the work Slack channel? All of these are questions your last boss probably didn't have to think about too hard. You do.

If that's not complicated enough, you also have to deal with the changing definition of professionalism—to paraphrase *The Princess Bride*, that word that does not mean what you think it means (at least, not anymore). Professionalism today is not the professionalism of our parents or grandparents. As the leader, you get to decide what it means for your team and your workplace.

Then we'll look outside of work to answer the question: How does your leadership persona extend to the internet, or alternatively phrased, what do you post on social media if your employees can see it? Is the internet boiling our brains and ruining our lives? (Yes.) Can we log off? (Not really. Or not without consequences, at least.)

Part two is about your team, your policies, and the culture you create.

We'll talk about what work is for (money, a sense of purpose, some modicum of dignity) and what it isn't for (basically everything else) and how next-gen leaders have to grapple with quickly changing expectations of the workplace. We'll get into the nitty-gritty of team culture and all the various ways remote work environments make it harder for us because, at this point, most places have some kind of remote/virtual component.

We'll talk about inclusivity and equity, how a no-assholes policy is hard to enforce but absolutely necessary, and how to deal with politics at work. Plus, some specific advice on how to create work-rest integration: vacation policies, a four-day workweek (!!), and family leave, for starters. Some of this will be harder to implement than other parts depending on your circumstances, but all of it is worth considering.

We'll also get into transparency—what it is, what it isn't, the challenges, the solutions for those challenges, and how hard it is to give the people what they want. Much like the responsibly authentic persona you're presenting, the key is to know who you are *as an organization*, who you're not, and how it affects the people you're leading.

Finally, in part three, we'll bring it back to you. Next-gen leadership is harder than ever before. Knowing that, how can we not just survive the work but actually thrive in it? We want our teams to not be miserable and to have space to be productive; we should set up the same structures for ourselves.

We'll dig in on how hard it is to be friends with the people you lead, how difficult and different networking is for next-gen leaders, and what you should really look for out of a mentor. We'll also touch on the importance of protecting your peace and finding your joy. The work is hard, but no one benefits when we're suffering for it.

Finally, we'll consider our collective ambition—what is it we want out of life, anyway? What do our careers look like now? (And why do so many of us struggle to explain to our grandparents what exactly it is we do all day?) What decisions can we make as leaders that allow us to think expansively about the future?

I'm not trying to describe what the current state of the workplace is, in part because so many workplaces are run by boomers and Gen X. Rather, this book is aspirational: What could it be like? What should leadership look like? What challenges will we face, and how can we tackle them? Especially as AI becomes more and more a part of our workplaces and lives, leadership will need to be even more human—and there will be an even bigger premium on authenticity. As our national political leadership gets even bleaker, the spaces we *can* control need to be even more carefully considered. We're going to need even more depth and empathy, more heart, and, just as critical, more boundaries. Doing it *right* doesn't mean it will be *easy*—in fact, doing it *right* will be incredibly challenging, and doing it *right* will look slightly different for each of us.

My hope is that you finish this book with a framework for how to choose your own adventure and that you do so with immense compassion for yourself, strong boundaries you can maintain, and an ever-expanding imagination for what could be possible.

* * *

I'm going to talk a lot in these chapters about my personal experience—so, let me introduce myself. A millennial born in 1990, I was raised in the edge of the Virginia suburbs of Washington, DC. I grew up on a steady pop-culture diet of Backstreet Boys and Britney Spears (and the ensuing body image issues of every teenage girl in the early 2000s), hundreds of Baby-Sitters Club books and the Dear America historical-fiction diaries—if you know, you know—and new episodes of *Friends* on Thursday nights.

I was in sixth grade on 9/11, voted for President Barack Obama the first time I was eligible to cast a ballot, and my first job after graduating college in 2012 was for his reelection campaign.

After a few other campaigns and political jobs, I cofounded Run for Something in 2017 and now serve as president of the multimillion-dollar organization, which recruits and supports young diverse leaders running for state and local office. We've built the largest pipeline of young leaders thinking about running for office on the left and have helped nearly two thousand people win elections across the country, transforming what civic leadership means in America.

I have always been a leader. I am a quintessential eldest daughter of four kids who are very close in age. Most of the time, I like being in charge. I have often found myself bracing against authority even in the smallest ways; a professor asking the class to take out a pen and paper would make me grit my teeth for no rational reason, whispering to myself, "Don't tell me what to do."

Whether it was producing the high school daily TV show, running production teams in the theater department, or taking on elected leadership roles in regional youth group—I have always sought out positions where I am setting agendas, delegating out tasks, and most important, getting other people fired up to do something that may feel objectively ridiculous but is critical to achieving our shared goal.

Case in point: As a sophomore in college outside Chicago, I took on the role of editor in chief of one of the bigger campus media outlets. I wasn't a journalism major, but I knew how to define success for my writers and was intentional about running a fun but productive newsroom. Most important, I wasn't afraid to say no when I needed to. I worked so hard I burned myself out, ultimately taking the winter and spring off to work at a magazine in LA.

When I came back my senior year, I immediately reverted to old habits and overloaded myself, alternating between writing my thesis for my degree in American studies, attending classes, taking on a role as chair of our senior-year committee, and getting an internship on President Barack Obama's reelection campaign, starting the process of fulfilling sixteen-year-old me's dream of working in politics.

My career ambitions came from a straightforward belief: I thought politics was an interesting and meaningful way to make the world a better place. Since I was in middle school, I'd spent various summers or semesters volunteering by knocking on doors, interning with my local Democratic Party office and on Capitol Hill, and learning through experience that the combination of art and science that goes into the campaign process appealed to me intellectually and emotionally.

After nine months working as an intern and finishing my degree, I was hired upon graduation as an email writer—at twenty-two and in an entry-level role, I was the most junior person on my team. Once again, a recurring theme: I worked around the clock (literally, getting into the office at 7:00 a.m. and often leaving well after 1:00 a.m.) to do something I believed in.

After we won the 2012 election, I stayed in Chicago and worked for a year as deputy email director for President Obama's newly formed nonprofit, Organizing for Action, which worked to build grassroots support for the president's agenda. I didn't have direct reports but helped lead the team of a half dozen people, handling project management and keeping the trains running on time. I adopted a dog and dipped my toes into the world of working hard but not working around the clock.

In 2014, I moved to Florida, where I got my first job as a people manager, with hiring and firing power, accountability, and all the good and terrible stuff that comes with it. I was the digital director for the Democratic candidate for governor, responsible for a multimillion-dollar budget for ads and consultants, a small team, and a handful of outside vendors and working directly with the former governor himself on his social media presence. We lost, so I went to Disney World and got so drunk I threw up at Epcot. It was, in a word, fine.

In early 2015 I moved to Brooklyn after I was hired to be the email director for Hillary Clinton's presidential campaign. I managed a team that grew to nearly two dozen people and, at twenty-five years old, was once again one of the youngest of my peers. For those of you not in the political sector, campaigns are wild. You are truly spending 24/7 with your employees and colleagues. There is no work-life balance because you have no time for life outside of work; there is similarly no time for management training or thoughtful leadership development. We obviously worked at work, but also drank at work, dated at work, and wept at work—it was messy, meaningful, and an incredible two years of growth for me as a leader, with the saddest possible ending.

That brings me to my current role. In 2017, just a few weeks shy of twenty-seven years old, I launched Run for Something with my cofounder, Ross Morales Rocketto. We recruit and support millennials and Gen Zers to run for local office. We started small, grew it big, and have made a meaningful impact on democracy and on thousands of communities across the country. We've directly shaped the country's definition of what a good leader looks like, both literally and in terms of vibes, by expanding access to information that was previously kept behind lock and key.

Throughout that, we've been building an organization that does incredible work while actively trying to treat our staff like real humans in an industry known for burning people out hard and fast. I've learned firsthand what it means to build and lead a diverse, fully remote team, as I've grown myself from a mid-twenties single woman and proud workaholic to a now-married thirty-something mom of two, who's more focused than ever before on balance and prioritization.

As cofounder and now president of the organization, I've had ups and downs. I've cried tears of joy as we won elections and grown bigger than my wildest dreams and sobbed just as many tears of anguish when we've struggled to barely make payroll, gotten rejected from major funding requests, and done drastic-but-necessary personnel cuts.

As I write this, I am deeply uncertain as to what the organization will look like when this book is published or in the years after that I hope you're reading it. There is a decent chance we're thriving. There's an equally decent chance we've closed down.

It hasn't been easy, and I haven't always gotten it right. Like so many people in positions of power, I've laid people off for financial reasons, fired people for cause, and disappointed people in countless ways. I have let down others and myself and inevitably failed to meet the values I've laid out.

I try to be honest throughout this book about my mistakes and what I've learned in an effort to make it clear that when *you* fuck up—which you will—you are not alone. I expect there to be critiques of my leadership, and those critics won't be wrong, but they won't be telling the full story, either.

I write about leadership knowing I am not a perfect example of a leader. I'm just a person, trying my best to do a thing in a way not many have tried before, with limited examples to take my cues from.

So let me say the bad stuff first, so you know who you're hearing from: I can be a bitch. I'm not patient when it comes to making time for small talk or doing the kind of greasing-the-wheels getting-to-know-you conversations that help build trust. I'm ultimately an introvert who pretends to be an extrovert for work. I curse more and rest less than I should. I don't always practice what I preach. I can be petty and I often hold grudges. I am not warm-touchy-fuzzy-feely, and I don't particularly care if people don't like me.

But I also know my strengths: I am clear-eyed about my mission and goals. I have always put the organization's imperatives first and my personal politics second, even when doing so requires me to shut the fuck up. I'm uncompromising about my intentions to build a people-first work culture, even if it doesn't always stick. I'm eager to push the existing norms within my industry on work-rest policies—including actively telling people, "No, seriously, stop working"—and to provide the best compensation we can afford. I barely take myself seriously, but I do take the work very seriously. I read every email I get. I'm good at remembering birthdays, I send flowers in tough moments, and when I RSVP yes to something, I show up.

This book is born from my personal experience as a leader, as well as my years spent working with hundreds of millennial and Gen Z politicians, whose public roles help shape the broader cultural idea of what a leader looks like. While it may not seem like politics translates to other industries, running for office can also be described as "asking other people to put their trust in you and your vision for the world," which is something leaders do both at work and outside of it.

But I also know that there's lots I don't know. So when I started my writing process, I put out a call for millennial and Gen Z leaders who were doing things differently and might want to talk about their experiences—I expected to chat with maybe two dozen folks total. Instead, I ended up interviewing nearly 130 leaders, ranging from their early twenties to early forties across a broad and diverse list of industries and sectors.

I talked to people like:

Jessica Barolsky, a millennial rabbi in Wisconsin, cancer survivor, and mom of two who described the challenges of taking over for a retiring rabbi who'd never taken a day off and used his Dictaphone to give notes to his assistant.

Ziad Ahmed, a Gen Z entrepreneur who ran a Gen Z–specific consulting firm that ultimately got absorbed by a major talent agency after we spoke. Ziad described the dance parties and vibe checks he ran at his company that helped cultivate the mood he wanted to facilitate.

Megan Sip, a millennial engineer at NASA, went in-depth on the ways she tried to navigate a male-driven industry.

Millennial Elizabeth Jackson-Rietz let me in on the internal branding and politics at Nike headquarters.

Annie Wu Henry, a Gen Z social media strategist and influencer, described the extreme career instability she experienced despite being seen publicly as a leader in her field.

Millennial delegate Adele McClure talked me through her own challenges as a working-class Black woman trying to find a "real" job while she served in the barely paid Virginia state legislature.

My interview subjects included doctors, scientists, teachers, artists, nonprofit executives, tech CEOs, writers, lawyers, politicians, influencers, and more. I talked with leaders with a broad range of backgrounds—people of different races, classes, industries, professional and personal experiences, and scales of work. (Throughout the book, I'll refer to people by the leadership roles they held at the time we spoke—like classic millennials and Gen Zers, many have since changed jobs.)

In those conversations, I asked every leader about how they described their leadership role and their leadership style—we talked about challenges they experienced, how they learned to lead, whether they felt they could "be themselves" at work, and more. I was amazed (but not surprised) at how many echoing themes there were across the interviews.

Whether I quote directly from those conversations or not, each one helped shape this book and opened my eyes to the kinds of challenges leaders today face. Similarly, I also read approximately one million (okay, sixtyish) leadership and management books in preparation to write this as well as for my own edification. Some of them were good! A lot of them were not. But all were helpful in illuminating how much leadership has changed over the years. For example, "management by walking around" is not a thing most of us can do anymore, if it ever really worked to begin with, and listing "toned" and "physically fit" as necessary traits of a good leader would perhaps raise some eyebrows. All that reading and those interviews reaffirmed for me: Next-gen leaders are working without a playbook. And if we try to keep following outdated rules set by the boomers and Gen X who came before us, we'll find ourselves more and more out of sync with our teams (and likely, ourselves).

• • •

Let's level-set. For the sake of this book, "next-gen" means millennials and Gen Z. Generally speaking, millennials are those people born between the early 1980s and the mid-1990s; Gen Z are from the mid-1990s into the early 2010s.

Obviously, that's a wide range! Generational divides are fuzzy, both between generations and within them—the experiences of an elder millennial born in 1980 and a young one born in 1995 are wildly different. Race, class, gender identity, sexual orientation, and location all intersect to shape an individual's own personal experience, abilities, and opportunities.

But academics have proved that generational divides not only exist but sustain over time. In particular, survey data taken over decades has shown that many of the attitudes cemented in one's youth and early adulthood tend to stay static as the generation grows up. Meaning, the way millennial and Gen Z leaders show up now foreshadows the way they'll show up in the future—their behavior is not just a by-product of these leaders currently being twenty- or thirtysomethings.

And because millennials and Gen Zers are the most diverse generations in American history, an increase in next-gen leadership hopefully directly correlates to an increase in leadership by people of color, LGBTQ+ individuals, women, and more. One key reason why next-gen leadership looks and sounds different is because next-gen leaders do not look or sound like the generally old white men who led before us, and are, generally speaking, leading more diverse teams than ever before.

Millennials are the first internet generation, the first truly multiracial, multiethnic generation, the generation who remembers 9/11 as a pivotal experience in our youth and who entered the workforce during or shortly after a financial crisis. We're marrying later, having kids later, buying homes later, taking on debt for longer, and jumping around jobs more. Unsurprisingly, all those things are connected and directly shape the values we bring to our leadership. According to the headlines, we're also cold-blooded killers, wiping out institutions like cable TV, department stores, canned tuna, beer, diamonds, the wedding industry, and golf.

Gen Z, meanwhile, is the first social media generation, growing up not just learning the internet but actually online themselves. Gen Z is even more racially diverse than millennials, broadly more progressive on many issues, and more demanding of a shared values system from the businesses they patronize. They are also, sadly, the school-shooting generation—they've been doing active shooter drills since kindergarten. Their mental health is all over the place, especially during and after the 2020 COVID pandemic. They have very few fucks to give, for lack of a better phrase, all of which affects how they show up in the limited leadership roles they've taken on so far. Their politics are rapidly changing—conventional wisdom on Gen Z's politics changed many times in the three years I spent working on this book—but those who have become leaders have already shown a new way of doing things, and the Gen Zers who take charge in the years to come will certainly blow things up in their own way.

As you read this, you may find yourself saying, "Leadership does not vary across generations; it's universal." In some ways, that's true. There are qualities that made a leader good during the Roman Empire that stand the test of time: honor, integrity, vision, an affinity for baths (probably). But there are indisputably some things leaders from past generations do—like legitimately use Facebook or care about visible tattoos—that are nearly impossible to imagine coming from a millennial or Gen Z leader.

Similarly, there are evolutions in the workplace itself—literally, like the technology we use, but also emotionally, as we grapple with changing expectations around the role work fills in our lives—that next-gen leaders have to deal with in a way our parents and grandparents would fundamentally not understand.

We also, candidly, have to deal with our peers: Millennials and Gen Z teammates are different than boomers and Gen X. Many of the challenges we have as leaders are in part because those we lead are grappling with the same mind-fucks around identity, technology, and more.

At the same time, I have some necessary caveats to set out:

Not all millennials, not all Gen Zers, not all boomers or Gen Xers, not all leaders, not all industries, not all geographies, etc. I simply can't speak for everyone. For example, there are millennial leaders who have boomer leadership styles, in part because they're modeling the bosses they've had before.

Furthermore, not every leader has the same kind of power. The CEO of a company has a different amount of influence than a mid-level manager; a PTA president has a different mandate than a nonprofit founder. There's a lot of nuance across leadership roles. If you read something and your reaction is "LOL I can't do that. I'm in charge but not that kind of in charge," that's okay! Maybe one day you will be. Or you can adapt in ways that make sense for your specific situation. Or maybe you can push the person *really* in charge to make a difference.

It's also worth being explicit: Not all leadership styles translate equally across every community—Black women leaders, for example, risk being penalized for being their authentic selves, while white men are often rewarded.

Finally, no generational leadership style is exclusively bad or exclusively good. Boomers have done good things (like ending wars), and next-gen leaders have done bad ones (like committing massive financial crimes). These generational leadership styles simply are what they are; sometimes they yield good outcomes, and sometimes they yield bad ones.

Of course, these generational leadership styles are also connected: Next-gen leadership is in direct conversation with boomer leadership.

Consider that the first leader most people encounter in their lives is a parent or guardian, and while the details and tasks may be different—writing a memo and changing a diaper both contain a certain amount of shit but are obviously not the same—boomer parenting and boomer leadership are remarkably similar.

As millennials and now Gen Zers become bosses (and parents), similar themes show up across both the professional and the domestic. Millennial parenting trends in particular—think gentle parenting and Big Little Feelings—are about teaching emotional literacy among our kids, setting and holding consistent boundaries, and creating space for them to become independent.

This may not resonate if you're not a parent, but replace the word "kid" with "employee" in the rest of this paragraph and you'll see what I mean: I am acutely aware that I am not my *kid*'s friend, nor their partner in crime. I am responsible for keeping my *kid* safe, fostering their development and independence, and setting clear boundaries for them to push on as appropriate and to thrive within. It's not my *kid*'s job to make me feel better or manage my emotions. It's their job to be a *kid*. Some things are just none of their business, and it's better for them that way.

In many ways, running an organization and dealing with a small child's roller coaster of emotions are the same, but one uses Google Docs and well-structured agendas while the other uses Daniel Tiger episodes.

Anne Helen Petersen, millennial writer—and thinker on all things millennial in particular—pointed out to me that part of the reason both millennials and boomers are like this is because the generations are, at their core, very similar. "Both boomers and millennials have incredible main-character energy," she said. "They dealt with significant shit over the course of their formative years" that really shaped how they approach adulthood. She noted economic stagflation of the seventies and eighties, Reaganomics, and the rising fetishization of the Christian right as just a few examples of how boomers had it tough. It's not exactly the same, she was clear—but it's also not *as* different as we might like to pretend.

The boomers and Gen Xers who came before us didn't have it easy. (No leader does!) But they didn't have to consider challenges like the internet, remote work, the changing expectations outside the workplace, and the emotional labor leaders are now expected to do. We're doing a hard thing in an even more difficult context.

• • •

If you've picked up this book, you're probably a millennial or Gen Zer looking for a leadership style that makes you feel comfortable in your own skin and who hasn't yet seen yourself reflected in any other resource.

If you're not a millennial or Gen Zer: That's okay! I'll preemptively ask for your forgiveness because I know those outside these generations might take offense to some of what I write. (I take offense at the lack of affordable housing and the increasing likelihood that my kids will have to fight in the water wars, so consider us even.) I'm going to use "we" to describe us next-gen leaders; don't take it personally if you don't identify accordingly. Consider this your field guide to understanding how leadership norms are shifting. If you're Gen X specifically: After the first edition of this book came out, I heard from a lot of you that you were mad you got ignored. (Classic Gen X response.) So let me apologize. You got just as screwed by boomers as the rest of us. Their stranglehold on power kept you out of the rooms where decisions were made. As of 2025, many major companies are going from boomer CEO to millennial CEO, skipping your peers over entirely. This is not your fault, and I'm sorry. You've got some of that next-gen screw-the-system bite in you, and for that, I appreciate you.

If you're not yet a leader: My hope is this book inspires you to want to lead yourself and gives you a framework for how to think about and prepare for the next step in your journey. I'm not going to ask you to have sympathy for your bosses—because I get it, they're the boss, fuck 'em—but hopefully you will finish this book with at least *some* empathy for the next-gen leaders in your life. It's really, really hard. By reading this, you're getting the shortcuts through the lessons many of us learned the hard way, so you go into your leadership role eyes wide open, knowing that the challenge before you is immense but that it is absolutely possible to lead without losing your humanity.

Think about ways you can incorporate the advice in this book into your work presence now. For example: Don't treat your work Slack like your group chat! What you write online can and will be seen by your employer (and, ahem, all your past and future employers)! You will be better off down the road if you start acting now the way you will when you're in charge.

If your leadership is outside of work: Great! When I say "team," I mean the people you influence. When I say "work," I generally mean the space your leadership role exists within. You could have one direct report; you could have one thousand people in your organization. Reporting lines could be clear, could be dotted, could be fuzzy—and it could be a volunteer effort, a pickup basketball game, a book club, whatever. Maybe the details about something like taking family leave aren't directly relevant to you, but consider how the underlying argument—that you should set things up so that, if needed, you can step away without your team losing focus—might apply for your role. Adapt as appropriate to your circumstances.

If you're already a leader: I hope this book gives you language to talk about the things you've struggled with. You should end this book feeling seen, reflected, and understood. What we are doing is unprecedented. It's not that you're a failure, it's that you're trying to do a really hard thing in a way few people have, and all the guides and examples available haven't quite hit the mark. I also hope you'll come away with some practical tools and considerations to incorporate into your leadership practice. (Like yoga, or music, or anything else that can never be fully perfected, it is a practice!)

If you're somehow none of those things: Thanks for reading.

PART ONE

If the questions include . . .

How do I be myself and also be in charge?

What does professionalism mean these days?

How do I post on social media when
my team can see it all?

The answer is:

By practicing responsible authenticity
and strategic communication at all times.

HOW TO BE YOURSELF (BUT RESPONSIBLY)

Next-gen leaders have been told our entire lives to "just be yourself!" and "be authentic!" We are told the secret sauce to success is to be vulnerable and honest; that the celebrities, influencers, and politicians who are described as "real" are the ones we should aspire to be like, often positioned in contrast to the public figures who seemed like they were created in a lab by industry puppet masters.

Then we're put into positions of power and quickly learn: We absolutely *cannot* be ourselves, at least not the way we've been taught or seen modeled for us online or in pop culture.

As leaders, our presentation matters. We are not the thermometer, reading the room—we're the thermostat, setting the temperature. If we decide to wear sweatpants and a tank top on Zoom calls (which I regularly do!), we're modeling what's acceptable for our team. If we show up every day in a full face of makeup and a fresh blowout, our team will think that's what's required. How leaders act shapes what everyone else will consider the group's norms.

In an interview on pop-culture podcast *Las Culturistas* in February 2024, Tina Fey told Bowen Yang words that went somewhat viral online and that stuck with me as the best possible embodiment of the challenges of being authentic as a next-gen leader:

"Authenticity is dangerous and expensive."

In a segment called "I don't think so, honey," where the guest talks for about a minute on a cultural phenomenon they dislike, Fey went on: "I regret to inform you that you are too famous," specifically cautioning *SNL* cast member and comedian Yang against giving his honest opinions on movies, something he'd done to help him grow his audience.

She warned him that the people he insults today may be his coworkers a few years down the road. He laughed, covered his face, and bashfully nodded.

You don't need to be famous, be on *SNL*, or host your own podcast for the same aphorism to apply to you. Authenticity *is* dangerous and *can* be expensive. That doesn't mean it's bad—in fact, authenticity is a necessary component of next-gen leadership—but if not wielded appropriately and intentionally, your "true self" can be your worst enemy.

That's because your job as a leader isn't to be your "true self"—it's to be your best *working* self in service of a mission. Your communication and self-presentation isn't really about you: It's about your goals and your team. You have to be yourself, but strategically.

Your task is to develop a responsibly authentic leadership *persona* that is directly drawn from who you are as a *person*. If your persona is a costume or mask you need to wear every day in all circumstances—like at work, for example—you want it to feel like a version of business athleisure, a metaphorical (or possibly literal) pair of pants that is put-together but still comfortable. Your persona shouldn't distract from your goals but also shouldn't make you feel like you're in an itchy costume or always faking it.

This is really hard to do: It can feel manipulative or calculating and, if poorly done, will come off as such. But if responsible authenticity is well executed, you, your mission, and your team will all be better off.

Part of the reason this (and all things next-gen leadership) is so hard is because we don't have a ton of examples.

Generally speaking, the boomer leadership style of "authenticity" has erred to one of two ends of the spectrum. On one end, there's the robot-boss-beep-boop machine who has no life outside of work, no personality outside of "boss," and no space for humanity. They are always on, always buttoned up, and always professional in the most traditional sense of the word. They do not make mistakes (and if they do, they do not own up to them), do not show vulnerability, and do not futz around with feelings. Boomer bosses would not dare to cry in the office because boomer bosses are probably men not particularly in touch with their emotions or women trying to emulate masculine leadership styles.

On the other end of the spectrum, there's the boomer boss who is the IRL embodiment of your great-aunt on Facebook—overemoting, oversharing, overpersonalizing. Their problems are your problems. Their bad morning or big fight with their spouse has consequences for your workday because their emotional-regulation skills are slim to none. You know about their IBS, their challenges quitting smoking, their stepdaughter's girlfriend's nose ring infection, their stresses and worries—you know it all, and you wish you didn't because you just want to get your work done and go home.

Meanwhile, as millennials and Gen Zers have come up through the ranks, we've been encouraged to live our truths. So many of us have been raised to embody utmost millennial-cringe sincerity or its Gen Z variation, no-fucks-to-give detachment. We've been told to be confident in our special-snowflake-ness and to bring our real selves with us, wherever we are and whatever that looks like. Consider Bowen Yang's challenge from earlier: His honest thoughts on movies and other pop-culture items are part of what furthered his career. Authenticity served him, up until it didn't.

I'll grant that some of this is, of course, a small- to medium-sized exaggeration. And yet: So many of the leaders I spoke with referenced past bosses whose inability or disinterest in self-regulation harmed group dynamics; others noted leaders or employees whose tendency to overshare put the entire team in a place of discomfort.

People in positions of power—any amount of power—need to be intentional about how we show up. Being perpetually #unfiltered does not always help us accomplish our goals nor serve our team. Being robots doesn't help us, either.

We want to be real people without putting too much of ourselves out there for our teams to have to manage around. We aspire to strike a balance somewhere between the two ends of the boomer spectrum. We don't want to be exhausted by the work of perpetually faking it, but we also don't want to put all our vulnerabilities out there for others to tear down—either option will eventually come back to bite us.

The solution is to find a safe landing spot. We must do the work of understanding who we are and who we need to be for our leadership roles and how to comfortably and consistently show up as the overlap between the two. I call this type of self-presentation "responsible authenticity," which may feel like a paradox, but bear with me as we work through it.

• • •

Authenticity is *the* buzzword in modern life. It's what people say they want out of celebrities, influencers, brands, politicians, and most relevant for this conversation, leaders. Leaders themselves say they want to embody it: In a study on executive presence—the ways bosses and leaders carry themselves in order to convey gravitas and power—37 percent of executives self-identified "authenticity" as a core communication skill.[1] This is all complicated by the introduction of AI, which has exploded in the years since I first started writing about this. Leaders who can genuinely connect as humans will be even more precious in a world where more and more is artificial—and at the same time, leaders with limited time will have to decide how to use AI as part of their self-presentation. This will get messy!

So what is authenticity? It's annoying to say this, but much like the Supreme Court said about porn, most of us know it when we see it.

One option for a definition for authenticity comes from OG shame and vulnerability researcher Dr. Brené Brown, who defines the term as "the daily practice of letting go of who we think we're supposed to be and embracing who we are."

I mostly like that definition—both because I'm a cliché white woman in my thirties who likes Brené Brown and, more important, because I think the definition of authenticity as a practice—as an active verb—is useful. Next-gen leaders have no choice but to let go of who we *should* be because so many of the models we've got for what leadership *should* be no longer work for us.

Another possible definition came from millennial writer Ann Friedman, who along with writing books and having run newsrooms over the years, runs her own newsletter, *The Ann Friedman Weekly*. She described authenticity using a metaphor:

> If you're lost in the mall, you don't run to every store looking for your mom. They tell you to stay in one place and your mom will find you. If you're running everywhere, trying to make something for potentially everyone, you may find no one. If you're in one place, being like I'm here, I'm doing me right here, people will find you.

If all that feels hard to pin down, consider defining authenticity by understanding inauthenticity. Even if we can't put our fingers on it, we can almost always tell when someone is bullshitting us. It can feel grating or even insulting.

Authenticity does not mean saying whatever you think or feel at any moment of the day. Authenticity does not forgive unprofessional behavior (although, as we'll get into shortly, what it means to be professional is rapidly shifting, so it needs to be made explicit and must be modeled by leadership). And authenticity is absolutely not an excuse for being an asshole.

Psychologist Adam Grant wrote in *The New York Times* back in 2016: "For most people, 'be yourself' is actually terrible advice."[2] He was right. Leaders who fuck up often use "I was just being myself!" as an excuse, in part because being your "real" self is often your most immature self. Saying whatever bullshit pops into your head might be what you consider authentic (and it is probably cathartic) but it's not always strategic toward your larger goals.

Beyond that, there is a certain amount of privilege that goes along with "being yourself"—it's too often used as an excuse for racism, sexism, or harassing others, for example. The people who believe they have permission to literally or figuratively let it all hang out are often those who feel that the normal rules don't apply to them. Don't be one of those people.

• • •

My personal journey around authenticity starts with a simple question: Who the fuck am I?

When I take online personality tests—as I recommend you do later in this chapter, and as one often does when procrastinating on real work—I tend to waver with each question: Do I answer this as my work self or my home self?

When I've got my leadership persona on, I am a professional extrovert: I can work a room, feed off the energy of the crowd, engage with the team, and leave the situation hyped. I'm specific, detail oriented, and rigorous—I am that person who catches the typo on page seventeen of the twenty-page memo. With my persona on, I am quick to give tough feedback, sometimes to my detriment. I'm collegial, even friendly, but I'm not the kind of person to proactively give hugs to my team.

I'm willing to do whatever is needed to accomplish our mission, even if it means making hard choices, upsetting others, or sacrificing my own comfort. I'll wake up at 3:00 a.m. to take the 6:00 a.m. flight to make the 10:00 a.m. meeting and will spend the flight home that evening emailing out follow-ups. The less kind interpretation of all that is probably "cold" or "indifferent to people's feelings," which I'll grant has some grain of truth to it. I have been told I celebrate accomplishments, not people.

Outside of my leadership role, I'm way more of an introvert—there is nothing I love more than time with my family, a book, and a patently absurd number of pillows and blankets. I'm (relatively) chill and way more forgiving of mistakes from my loved ones. My dog is not what you would call a "good dog," in part because I'm a pushover when she wags her dumb little tail at me and wants a treat. I'm exceedingly silly and, in my most trusting relationships, very affectionate.

The question is: Which is the real me?

The answer is: It actually doesn't matter. What matters is that I can adopt my leadership persona consistently—which is much easier when it's built on the core parts of who I am.

My goal is not to be 100 percent myself all the time; my goal is to regularly be the leader version of myself when it's required and to do so in a way that's sustainable for my mental health—and the best way to do that is for the leader version of me to be in alignment with my values and my goals, both personal and professional.

If I have to put only the tiniest bit of effort into the performance of the leader version of me, I am more likely to do it over and over again. That consistent behavior is what builds trust between me and my team.

So when I draw the Venn diagram of my various selves, I get a pretty good sense of where the overlap is: All versions of me are goal oriented and unyielding when I decide to set myself at something, whether it's a work project or determining exactly how to convince my toddler to brush her teeth (although parenting has been a real-time and likely lifelong lesson in giving up control). No matter the context, I am aggressive about communication and transparency—even if my husband doesn't necessarily *require* that I live-text him as I grocery shop, I'll do it for entertainment and accountability.

I feel strongly about showing up when it counts—if I'm invited and I can make the logistics work, I will always go to the meeting, the birthday party, or the funeral, and I will try my hardest to be on time. I am a problem solver to a fault, even if that's not always what's called for at the moment.

The manifestation of me may shift, but the core me is still me. Forgive me for speaking in third person, but: The book of Amanda is always the same, but the book cover can change depending on whom I'm selling it to.

The challenge for me, and for so many next-gen leaders, comes in part from the flattening of that divide between work self and home self. Whereas actors and politicians perceived as authentic in their public personas are actually just turning it on when the spotlight is on them, and while boomers might have been able to leave their work selves at work, next-gen leaders have to perform ourselves, whatever that means, in every possible space and platform: in Slack, on Instagram, over Zoom, at retreats, in one-on-one meetings, and in front of big rooms of people. We are always a little bit (or fully) on the clock, and we have to carefully curate ourselves at all moments.

I was not surprised that when I asked next-gen leaders if they felt they could be their real selves with their teams, they said something along the lines of "Well, kind of." (At least one person memorably said, "Fuck no.")

Some felt they needed to be chameleons, adapting their management and communication styles to what best fit their teams. Others expressed an obligation to hold some things close, knowing that it's not the responsibility of their employees to manage their relationships.

Others still explained their personas allow them to have the space to make the hard but necessary decisions that come with responsibility, create some distance between them and the inevitable criticism, and give them the tools to better distinguish between helpful feedback and the standard bitching and moaning.

For those who further deviate from the "traditional" understanding of what leaders look like (interpret that in this context as not white, not male, not straight, not cisgender, and/or not disabled), we *really* don't have permission to say, do, or act however we truly feel.

Jenn Stowe, the millennial executive director of the National Domestic Workers Alliance, told me, "As a Black woman, I have to pay attention to the way that I show up, in the way that I'm authentic in my leadership. Oftentimes, Black women can't bring their whole selves to work—I bring my best self to work and bring the person that the staff needs, that allows me to lead well and be positioned well—I think I can do that without being fake."

She described the nonwork version of herself as her "Saturday self"—the version of her that hangs out at home with her family—and explained that bringing her Saturday self to work was "not a choice that [Black women] have."

I heard this from so many of the leaders of color I spoke to, who talked either explicitly or implicitly about facing "double jeopardy," the phrase minted by Black feminist and activist Frances M. Beal to describe the racism and sexism experienced by Black women and women of color more broadly.[3] These leaders felt encouraged to be themselves but penalized if they were *too* themselves, with fuzzy lines and unclear expectations about what any of that actually meant in practice.

This all sounds overwhelming and exhausting. It is. More so than nearly anything else, the responsibility to always be goal oriented is what makes leadership so hard, whether we're at the top of the pyramid or middle managers. We have to bite our tongues, eat the shit sandwich, or as someone once jokingly told me in a not-so-inspiring-but-ultimately-comforting moment: put our dignity in a box and revisit it later.

Self-regulation is one of the most essential parts of responsibly authentic leadership: We have to adjust our behavior to the spaces and places we're in because leadership is not solely, or even primarily, about us feeling comfortable; it's about our teams and our goals. At every point, we need to be clear about what we're trying to accomplish and, when considering our self-presentation, ask ourselves: Does this get us *as a team* closer or further away from that goal?

People, especially millennials and Gen Zers, say they want authenticity out of their leaders. I gently and respectfully suggest those people are (unintentionally) full of shit.

Stepping back, most people don't actually want leaders to be ourselves, because it's not really about us. People want leaders to create space for *them* to be *themselves* by cultivating two specific feelings:

1. **Trust.** People want to know that expectations and reality are aligned—they want to be able to be both confident in and comforted by structure and to know that when they are told something, they can believe it.

2. **Psychological safety.** People want to feel like *they* can be themselves (or a version of themselves) without risk of physical or emotional harm.

So what do we as leaders actually *do* to create those feelings? So glad you asked.

It's a two-part answer: first, how we behave as individuals (which we'll get into shortly), and second, the kinds of policies and structures we set up (which we'll get into in part two).

• • •

As leaders looking to tactically understand how an individual practices authenticity, the most obvious example is the influencer.

Influencers *are* a form of leaders—on most platforms, they literally have followers, but beyond that, they are doing what leaders do: building a relationship with a community over time in order to drive a desired action.

Maybe the influencer wants their followers to buy something, maybe they want them to take action, maybe they want them to cyberbully someone else on the internet. The end goal is (mostly) irrelevant for our purposes. It's more useful to focus on what the influencer is doing with each post and each interaction in order to build their most important currency: trust.

That relationship between influencer and follower is cultivated over time, with consistency and transparency (or performed transparency) so that the audience knows what to expect from the influencer. The influencer's power is literally derived from the large number of people who trust them and take cues from them.

Jordan Harrod, a Gen Z STEM content creator and PhD student, explained that she thinks of her online self as a role she's performing—literally, when her content started taking off a few years in, she took an acting and improv class.

"What does she look like on camera? What kind of things does she post about?" she told me, explaining how she considered the character of "Jordan Harrod, Content Creator."

"I change into different clothes, I'm doing my hair a little bit differently—I'm getting into costume to be this person. And then when I'm done, I can change back into what I normally wear and become normal me again."

As her accounts grew over the years, she had to step back and ask herself: "How much of myself do I want to give to this? How do I draw the line between the me that is portrayed publicly and the person that I actually am?"

That process of definition has required intentionality. She's had to constantly renegotiate the boundaries of the character she was playing without molding it to be too far away from who she really is. Jordan hasn't shied away from being honest on her accounts, posting content over the years about struggling with her mental health and grappling with a diagnosis of ADHD. But she has been careful about when she brings those things into the public eye.

"My rule for sharing things about my personal life is that it has to have happened at least six months ago. If there's something happening that I'm still working through, I tend not to bring it up," Jordan explained because she (understandably!) has no interest in the internet's input on something she's still personally processing.

She's still herself in her content, but she explained, "There's a dial." For the industry-conference version of herself, when she's giving talks related to her PhD in medical engineering and medical physics, she dials it all the way up; for her main YouTube channel, she's at maybe 20 percent amped, whereas for Twitter and Instagram, maybe she's at 10 percent. She's calibrating based on audience—the core of the brand is still her, but the performance of it varies.

If you're too cool for school and don't follow influencers, congrats, you're more highbrow than nearly everyone else on the internet. But if you're like the rest of us, open up your social media platform of choice. Instagram is probably the easiest one, but if you're not on there or it no longer exists when you're reading this, pick another platform, or ask a search engine or AI robot to find you an influencer.

Specifically, look for someone who does social media for a living—someone who has explicitly monetized their account in order to support themselves either fully or partially and whose subject is themselves. Think: lifestyle influencer, parent influencer, fashion, food, fitness—any of those work. For the sake of this exercise, an influencer who does unboxing of products, gaming, or content reviews probably isn't as useful.

Scroll or tap through and evaluate them, not as a follower or fan but rather as a critical consumer.

A few questions to consider as you peruse:

- Which five or six words would you use to describe the influencer's brand, and why?

- Which parts of their life are they revealing online, and what do you notice is conspicuously missing?

- Look at the visuals: Is there a color palette or image gradient they tend to use? Are they dressed a certain way? How do they curate their appearance?

- Consider the audio: Are there music or sounds that repeat themselves? Is it heavy on the voice-over? Are they tapping into trends or making their own?

- Contemplate the text: Are they heavy into emojis? Are there long captions, or is brevity valued? Is there profanity? Jargon? Who is the likely audience they're writing for?

- Follow the money: How often do they engage with sponsored content or ads? How is paid content different from their "normal" content?

- Expand your scope: Who else online do they follow or engage with in a way you can see? Do they mess around in the comments? How much are they showing you behind the curtain? How do they seem to be cultivating community among their followers?

No matter how much an influencer tells us they're being 100 percent real or giving us the nitty-gritty, it's all a performance—even the stuff that they insist isn't a performance is a performance. They're capitalizing on being "relatable" (or intentionally stepping beyond relatability, e.g., the Kardashians) and in order to accomplish that, they need to make intentional, curated choices.

I think about this constantly, as I'm in the stage of life where I consume a lot of parenting internet. When I come across a video of a new mom doing a "day in the life with my baby" and complaining about their baby that won't sleep, I often find myself talking back to the content creator: Maybe it's because they're a baby just being a baby, but also maybe it's because you're shining a ring light in their face in the middle of the night! Put the camera away and let that baby rest!

Every single thing the influencer has presented to you is a choice, from which photo they post to what they're wearing in that photo to the caption they include, which hashtags are appended, and which other accounts they do or do not tag in the process. Their authenticity is curated. That doesn't mean their online personas are not grounded in truth. It just means they're not the *full* truth.

That's the real takeaway here. As a leader, you benefit from being *perceived* as authentic—that may require dialing up or dialing down how much of yourself you present, all in service of your goal. Think of your leadership persona or style as the way you'd write your influencer brand summary. What would you look like? How would you sound? Which parts would you share, and what would you keep private? How do you make those decisions?

Your task is to be *responsibly authentic*. That may sound like I'm telling you to be an overly calculating maniac who treats every day like an improv class gone wild.

I'm not. I'm imploring you instead to center the idea that all communications are strategic communications—if you're not intentional about what you're modeling for your team, you could be undermining your ultimate goal.

• • •

The process of designing your responsibly authentic leadership persona is kind of like picking out an empty place to live. Your home could be an apartment, a townhome, a big house, an RV, a tent, a van; it could be made of bricks or metal or red plastic fit for a troll doll—there is no objectively right or wrong answer, only the answer that feels good to you and fits your needs.

The persona-development process involves three steps: (1) Be clear about who you are, (2) be precise about what you want to accomplish, and (3) define the overlap between the two.

Then, as we'll get into in the next chapter, you'll decide how to show that off: how to dress, how to sound, how to communicate in various forms, and more. Or, to extend our house metaphor, you have to determine what your decorating style is, what your furniture looks like, and what colors you paint the walls.

But first, let's build the house.

STEP 1:
Who are you?

In order to perform authenticity, you have to first understand who you are. You can't develop a persona without knowing who you are as a person. This can feel a little navel-gazing or introspective in a way that not everyone finds comfortable, but it is an unavoidable part of the process.

One way to go about figuring this out, if you're not sure where to start: Answer the following three questions five different ways—as if the person asking is (a) a possible employer, (b) your best friend, (c) your parent, (d) your archnemesis, or (e) a stranger on the street.

1. What do you care about?

2. What gives you joy?

3. What makes you angry?

What stays true across those answers? What changes, depending on who's asking?

In her excellent book *The Art of Showing Up: How to Be There For Yourself and Your People*, Rachel Wilkerson Miller suggests breaking down exactly what makes you *you* by doing a deep inventory on your core values and priorities.

Miller explains that everyday decisions, "how you get to school/work, the foods you eat, the clothes you buy and wear, who you spend time with . . . how much time you spend on your phone and what specifically you're doing on it" are all representations of your values.[4] Use your preferred search engine to find lists of core values if you don't have any concrete ideas, and identify the ways in which those nouns shape your verbs.

Miller also suggests doing icebreakers with yourself—again, you can search the internet for lots of suggestions on get-to-know-you questions both serious and silly. You can also take personality quizzes, which, as you know, I find very stressful but can be kind of fun (or at least make for good group-chat fodder). All this is in service of self-reflection—the answers are less important than the process of interrogating who you are and what you know about yourself.

Think through your last week. When did you feel most like yourself? Think about the moment you were able to just unclench your jaw, let your shoulders drop, unbutton that top button of your pants—whatever your physical manifestation of relaxation is. Think about the moment when you didn't have to carefully contemplate every single word that came out of your mouth and could just speak freely. What were you doing, who were you with, what about it felt like you?

Now, describe the version of you from that moment. Describe *that* person's behavior, how they act, how they dress, the type of language they use. This will feel like an out-of-body experience. It is! Don't worry, you'll reincorporate shortly.

Come back to your leadership role. What about the box you're trying to fit into as a leader chafes against that relaxed version of you? Where is the conflict? Where is the tension? Naming it doesn't necessarily make it go away but will ultimately help you work through it.

After doing all this, you should by now have an exhaustive mental note (or even a written-down one or a voice memo, if you prefer) about who you are. Put it down for a week—set yourself a calendar reminder to return to this thought experiment.

When that calendar reminder comes back up, ask yourself: Does your description still resonate?

Set it aside for another week and consider it again. Has anything changed?

Bake this process into your life for the foreseeable future—you don't need to evaluate this every week, but maybe every three months, or every six, or once a year around your birthday, whatever feels the most comfortable. Change is good! Being too rigid about your sense of self can actually inhibit your growth. You're allowed and encouraged to change (and hopefully improve) as time passes. As long as you're aware of the changes and incorporate them into your own self-narrative, you're golden.

One final step in self-reflection ironically involves someone besides yourself: Ask someone or multiple someones for honest feedback about your presentation of self. This often comes up in the context of media training—a process that lots of leaders go through when learning how to work with reporters or show up in public spaces (and I highly recommend it). I went through one such session early on when we started Run for Something, and the most valuable piece of feedback I got was "Do not frown when the reporter asks you a stupid question."

"Even when the question is really stupid?" I asked, only kind of joking.

"Even when the question is *really* stupid," the communications expert confirmed, taking my rebuttal seriously. Practicing that skill has taken so much effort over the years. My authentic reaction remains an "are you fucking kidding me" face (and sometimes when it serves my goals or is appropriate, I show it); my responsibly authentic reaction is a more restrained pivot away from whatever dumb shit is being posed to me, often with a "What an interesting question! I think the real topic at hand is" response that leads into my actual communication goals.

This part sucks. You need to ask people what's the good and the bad of working with you, and you need to listen when they tell you. If you can, try to find folks who no longer have skin in the game—former team members who ideally left on good terms are strong possible participants, since they'll have way fewer incentives to kiss your ass.

If your only option is current teammates, well, ask anyway. Whether or not they're honest is a separate question, but at the very least: You should try! The appearance of seeking honest feedback matters just as much as actually receiving it.

What you hear in response may be genuinely helpful, or it may hurt your feelings. Either way, don't take it personally. I won't spout the cliché that all feedback is a gift—not all gifts are appreciated, nor are they all given in good faith—but it can be useful to consider those responses as data points in your broader understanding of who you are.

STEP 2:
What are you trying to accomplish?

A responsibly authentic leadership persona lives in the overlap between two key components: (1) who you are, and (2) what you're trying to do. We've got the first step down; now let's lock in on step number two: What are your goals?

Answer this extremely literally. What are you leading your team to? What are you trying to accomplish? What behavior are you hoping to model for your people?

There are approximately one billion guides online and in other management books that will walk you through how to set goals—SMARTIE ones (Specific or Strategic, Measurable, Ambitious or Achievable, Realistic or Relevant, Time-Bound or Timely, Inclusive, and Equitable) or the Four Ps (Positive, Personal, Possible, and Prioritized) or WOOP (Wish, Outcome, Obstacle, and Plan) or any other acronym or mnemonic device you might find.

The gist of all of them is straightforward: You need to be clear about what you're trying to get done, what could get in your way, and why it all matters.

Your goal could be to make lots of money (just define what "lots" is, by when, and for whom) or run the best PTA in the world (again, just define what "best" looks like, how you're measuring it, at what points, and whom you are comparing yourself to). The more details the better. You want a clear mission statement so that, when things come up, you have a North Star that gives you a framework for saying, "Yes, this serves our mission," or, "Nope, super doesn't."

Millennial Florida state representative Anna Eskamani described that one of the common pitfalls of being a new leader is the inability to discern between tactics and goals. Since getting elected in 2018 in a tough-to-win district in Orlando, Anna has been one of the leaders of the progressive fight in the scary-red (for now!) state, operating from the inside of the state legislature as much as she can, while coordinating organizers and activists outside to apply additional pressure when appropriate.

"Holding a protest should not be your goal," she explained, as an example of where she sees less experienced but very passionate activists missing the mark. "A protest is a tactic to get an issue in the media or push a decision-maker," not an end in and of itself.

Applied to herself, Anna has determined her goal is to advance progressive values and policy solutions that make life better for people. She intentionally stays away from deeper leadership roles in the party infrastructure itself so that she can leverage being "outside" strategically. Anna's had to fight against "other people's ambitions" for her, including pushing her to run for a higher office that might put her into conflict with someone she likes and respects. "Don't have an ego," she says, albeit knowing that's easier said than done. With a clear mission statement for herself, she can fend off the siren call of other things that might be short-term appealing but long-term self-defeating.

Evan Spiegel, millennial CEO and cofounder at Snap Inc., puts it simply for his context: "We are running a business. There is no drift from that clarity—especially for us, serving a community of eight hundred million people. We put that front and center. We're trying to help them connect with their friends and family—we've got to do that in the best way we can," he said.

That clarity allows him to design his leadership style in a way that's strategic and goal oriented. He shows up as the responsibly authentic version of himself that serves that purpose, balancing his empathy for his teammates—which is a core value to his sense of self—with a clear-eyed focus on the outcomes, and when he has to have a hard conversation, outcomes must come first.

STEP 3:
Who do you need to be?

This is the final piece of developing your persona. You've got the core pieces of (1) who you are and (2) what you want to accomplish—now you have to define the crossover.

What does your mission require of you? Who does your team need you to be?

I think about this the way I think about social media: The LinkedIn version of me (professional!) and the Instagram version of me (mostly books and dog pics!) and the Twitter/X version of me (snark and politics!) and the Facebook version of me (at this point mostly big life updates every eighteen months!) are all me, just different sides of me, specifically shared with the audience and purpose of the platform in mind.

None of that is a lie. It's just strategic and intentional, as all communications should be.

Bringing this dial-up dial-down approach into real life, and especially into the workplace, can get more complicated—especially when you're trying to model vulnerability without crossing boundaries or putting responsibility onto folks who cannot or should not shoulder it.

Your problems are not their problems: Max Lubin, a millennial nonprofit founder, experienced a common example of this. His organization, Rise, was focused on making higher education accessible and affordable by building students' political power—most of his team were other millennials and Gen Zers. Max started the organization when he was just twenty-seven and set out explicitly to create the kind of boundaries that his previous bosses had always blown up.

It was hard. Many members of his team were brand-new to the workforce, and many had finished college remotely during the pandemic and never had an in-person job before. "We thought we were just going to be teaching folks how to do advocacy and organizing. It was more remedial than that: They needed lessons on how to be professional," he explained, even while understanding that professionalism had changed. "Basic stuff—how to show up on time, be accountable, and occasionally more extreme stuff like how to not vape on a Zoom call," he said, and teaching staff that "you can't have sex with your coworkers—or please, don't have relationships that can't pass a basic HR test."

He sighed. The challenges were exacerbated when, in the summer of 2020, he started experiencing intense panic attacks. He sought treatment from doctors and confided in loved ones, but he went back and forth between letting coworkers in on what was going on or, as he put it, "just keeping that shit to myself and trying to work it out."

He ultimately chose to keep it private, concluding that it's not his employees' responsibility to worry about his health—it's their responsibility to do their jobs.

"I thought about experiences that I'd had earlier in my career where my bosses overshared or overstepped boundaries in ways that were not appropriate and ultimately made me responsible for them in a way that, like a parenting dynamic, can get inverted. So I've tried to model the kinds of boundaries I wanted my team to have." He explained, "Being an authentic leader does not mean I tell my employees everything that's going on with me."

Boundaries are good, actually: Comedian/activist/producer Ilana Glazer, creator of many things but, perhaps most famously, the quintessential millennial series *Broad City*, told me about the personal journey she went through defining her boundaries—while her stand-up and writing used to include personal anecdotes, she's now enjoying not including her personal life in her work. She explained that for her, "authenticity does not mean sharing personal things about yourself. . . . Being the authentic leader is holding your shape [while serving as] that leader."

She has to know herself in order to hold that sense of self—she credits lots and lots of therapy for that self-awareness—and can now better serve her team and her ultimate goal of creating interesting and engaging art by not yielding. While making and promoting a movie entirely about pregnancy and motherhood, Ilana kept strong boundaries around how she talked about or exposed her daughter. She could draw from the experience she was having as a new mom while not crossing a line about how she brought her kid into the limelight.

Technology can both muddle and enable these boundaries: Lisa Conn, millennial founder and CEO of Gatheround, a virtual-meeting technology tool, explained that she's further refined her boundaries after crossing them: "I'll post on close-friends Instagram stories, 'I'm stressed today!' And three members of my team will Slack me and be like, 'Are you okay?'" And she has to clarify: It's because her kid's sick, not because of work.

She does share parts of herself publicly and is willing to be vulnerable: Lisa made headlines in 2023 when she posted a photo of herself breastfeeding her infant during a work call that ended up going megaviral, attracting both positive attention and intense misogynistic and sexist commentary. The posting of the photo may not have been intentional—she just thought it was a nice picture of her new life as a working mom—but the way Lisa handled the ensuing attention was. She used it as a moment to bring business in, encouraging companies to consider remote work that enabled flexibility for parents (and that could be better serviced by her virtual meeting platform!).

Lisa describes her personal MO as "edited humanity," with transparency about the things that she thinks are important for her team to model. Her calendar is public and includes things like exercise, doctor's appointments, mental health, and other ways of caring for herself. But she notes, "I definitely have to edit the real talk because of the power it has," and that, like so many of the people I talked to, she's had bosses who would do "emotional dumping," constantly oversharing what they were struggling with, burdening their direct reports in the process.

Similarly, I leverage my calendar as a way of providing transparency into who I am as a person outside of work: My calendar is almost entirely visible (with some exceptions for HR-related meetings or truly confidential conversations), and includes blocks for therapy, exercise, and childcare responsibilities. I fully acknowledge, as the boss, I have more baked-in flexibility than some members of my team, but I don't do anything myself I wouldn't accept from any of them.

A necessary caveat: This has absolutely gotten harder as the company has grown, and more transparency doesn't always serve the team (a tension we'll come back to in part two), but at the very least, I can model the behavior I want to see from others and hold myself accountable for practicing what I preach.

That's the underlying premise of all this: Bring as much of yourself to work as you want to see from your team in a way that serves your goals. That means you have to be intentional about it all: how you dress, how you sound, which topics you speak on and where, all of it—all while navigating the boundaries of norms that have been shifting rapidly under our feet around "professionalism."

REDEFINING PROFESSIONALISM

The definition of professionalism has changed. This is not a hot take; it's just a fact. The question for next-gen leaders is: What do we do with that?

Some things have remained consistent across nearly all generations and contexts: Professionalism still includes things like general etiquette (e.g., say please and thank you; you're not a monster), respecting someone else's time, giving someone the dignity of having your full attention when they ask for it, and other core facets of how we interact with one another because we live in a society.

At the same time, the definition of professionalism (especially the aesthetics of it) has wildly changed in ways that blow boomers' minds.

It used to be that having tattoos or nose rings or bare shoulders was unprofessional—now, in most contexts, who cares? Cursing used to be unprofessional—now it's a sign of relatability. Emojis weren't even part of most Americans' vernacular a decade-plus ago; now they're almost akin to a second language, with their own context-specific definitions.

Navigating these waters of self-presentation may make you feel a little lost (or, more drastically, send you spiraling into an identity crisis) as you try to close the gap between person and persona. Being "professional" as it was previously defined and seeming "authentic" as is currently demanded can seem situated at opposite ends of the spectrum—that's because, up until relatively recently, they were.

But next-gen leaders are changing that in real time. We are collectively redefining what it means to be ourselves and also be in charge. We're figuring out what it means to be honest about our mental health challenges while not burdening our employees with our problems, how to model having lives outside of work while not overexposing ourselves, how to look like a boss without needing to feel like we're wearing a costume every day.

This isn't easy. But it matters: The way you dress, the words you use, the way you participate in Slack—it all sets the tone for what is acceptable in your team and what you deem appropriate or not. As the leader, you are the ultimate culture bearer for your community. The way you show up demonstrates to your team how they can show up and how much of themselves they can bring to work with them.

This kind of careful cultivation of a leader persona can feel like trickery or like hiding your true self from others in order to use them. I prefer the way Raena Boston, a millennial HR professional and cofounder of Chamber of Mothers, an advocacy group for moms, explained it: "I don't think everybody's entitled to my vulnerabilities. . . . Not everybody's earned that right to me."

It's good to have boundaries about which parts of yourself you offer up for consumption—it's net positive, both for you and your team. Because, repeat after me again, and again, and again: Your leadership isn't about you. It's about *them.*

In the previous chapter, we developed a responsibly authentic persona—the foundations and framework for our sense of self-presentation. Maybe we went full brick and mortar or maybe we preferred the tree house model; it doesn't matter. In this chapter, good news, HGTV fans, we get to talk decorating. We'll get into how you make decisions about your appearance and the way you communicate across a multitude of platforms in order to serve your goals.

• • •

This starts with dress codes. The way you dress and present yourself visually is unfortunately part of the deal.

This was a bit easier for leaders who came before us. Business suit or pencil skirt, formal shoes, muted colors, and they could call it a day.

That's no longer the case. Workplace formality has been sliding toward casual for decades—the pandemic and accompanying transition to remote work, whether temporary or permanent, hit the hard reset button on what dress was appropriate for professionals and leaders.

There are certainly some who still insist on button-down shirts and blazers over Zoom calls, but for many, the shift to appearing through a rectangle on a computer screen instead of an office allowed for some modicum of freedom of expression.

A few years removed from the era of "no hard pants," coincidentally coinciding with the rise of the next-generation leaders like us, the norms about professional dress and what's appropriate for leaders continue to evolve. While a decade of data shows a stable one-third of leaders still believe a "polished look" is important for executive presence, what "polished" means has shifted—in 2012, 13 percent pointed to "next job style of dress" (meaning that old axiom of dressing for the job you want, not the one you have), whereas 22 percent of leaders in 2022 pointed to the "new normal style of dress."

This is true regardless of gender identity. Facebook founder Mark Zuckerberg's black T-shirts and crypto scammer Sam Bankman-Fried's hoodies, as examples of the millennial-tech-bro "uniform," are chosen affectations intended to communicate a sense of informality and IDGAF-ness—a visual response to the business suit of the olden days. The reverse is also true: Zohran Mamdani campaigned in a suit—no matter the context—because it helped him undercut an argument that he was not serious enough.

But for a moment, I want to focus on women, who have it particularly tough as we take on positions of leadership, often as the first or only of our communities to do so, and grapple with entering spaces not meant for us.

Tiana Epps-Johnson, the millennial cofounder of the Center for Tech and Civic Life, one of the leading nonpartisan nonprofits protecting democracy and defending elections across the country, has a uniform: She regularly wears her hair in a bun on the top of her head with a thick stretchy headband wrapped just behind her ears, showing off giant gold hoops. I asked her if that was intentional.

"It's *so* intentional," Tiana said. "I once met a Black woman who was a [professional] fundraiser, and she told a story about how she was coached to never wear big gold earrings when doing fundraising because folks would find it tacky and low-class. So I only fundraise in gold hoops," she said with a big smile. "Sometimes I'll do a different big earring, but they'll always be something [someone else might characterize] as cheap."

Tiana has raised literally over half a billion dollars to support local-election administration offices' efforts to modernize and deal with growing challenges and is one of the country's leading democracy defenders and advocates. She gave a wildly well-received TED Talk in two-inch-thick platform boots and a classic skater-girl dress, telling me, "You don't have to wear a pair of heels or any other thing to feel like you belong on a stage like that."

In West Virginia, millennial state legislator Kayla Young's gone through a journey when it comes to how she presents herself. During her first campaign in 2022, she decided she was going to have a uniform, full stop, so she didn't even have to think about it.

"I'm just going to be the jumpsuit person," she declared, describing the six differently colored but otherwise identical jumpsuits she bought to wear through her campaign. "This is going to be my thing." And it was! Until she got elected and realized she couldn't wear that on the floor of the State Capitol.

So she showed up on her first day as a state legislator in a suit and sneakers—nice ones, fun ones, she clarified, but sneakers all the same—and the sergeant at arms tried to call her out.

She told him, "Show me where it says I can't wear those," and she pulled up the rules. She went on against the sergeant: "See all those guys' shoes? Those are all sneakers, too. Don't try to kick me off the floor. Let's see what happens."

She got to keep her sneakers on and has since found her own sense of fashion on the floor—she described a pair of metallic leather pants (that I really want to find) paired with a tweed blazer that was both professional and fun, matching the energy she brings to her leadership.

Kayla is also covered in gorgeous tattoos, including on her legs and on the palm of her hand—while she's proud of her body art, she's careful about how much she reveals them when she's in public and especially on the State Capitol, where she puts on fleece-lined tights that cover her legs entirely, both to protect her from the extreme air-conditioning and to stop her colleagues from wanting to talk to her about her ink. "I'm just sick of talking about it," she says. "We have work to do."

Tiana's and Kayla's wardrobe choices speak to the importance of being intentional about what you wear. You don't have to dress the way older leaders did to be taken seriously, but you want how you look to be integrated into the larger persona you're presenting.

That could mean you have signature looks like Kayla's jumpsuit or Tiana's hoops. Maybe you're always the most fashionable person in the room, or maybe your clothes are totally unremarkable in the sense that they're not worth remarking on. Neither option is right or wrong. What you don't want is for your appearance to make you feel like you're wearing a costume that doesn't fit or for your clothes to distract from rather than further your mission.

So, how do you figure out what to wear and how to look when the norms are changing and there's no single professional dress code anymore?

I won't give you specific fashion advice—clothing and makeup are not my strengths, to put it lightly.

But I will toss out a few questions for you to consider as you think about how you present yourself visually.

- Which clothes, hair, and physical features make you feel the most like yourself? If you had absolutely no restrictions, what would you wear?

- Do you want to stand out or blend in?

- How much thought do you want to put into any of this? Does picking out clothes and dressing yourself bring you joy, or does it bring you anxiety?

- What matters functionally for what you do? Are there physical requirements for your role that your appearance needs to take into account?

- If your leadership role requires any amount of videoconferencing: How does what you're wearing and how you're presenting yourself come off on camera?

- What are your financial and practical realities? Do you have budgetary constraints around what you can or want to spend on your clothes? How easy or hard is it to find clothes in your size?

Practically, lots of leaders I talked to mentioned renting clothes as a way to be both cost-effective and on trend, which is an excellent option if you can avail yourself of it. Others referenced a uniform, which took the decision fatigue out of the process—I certainly lean in that direction, learning by experience there is no limit on the number and variety of black jumpsuits and bright-red lipsticks one person can rotate through.

One final hot tip: Don't sleep on the value of a good tailor. Clothes that fit make a huge difference, no matter how much they might have cost off the rack.

As long as your clothes do two things—(1) make you feel like the best, most confident version of yourself and (2) don't detract from your goals—they're the right clothes to wear.

• • •

Next-gen leaders also have to grapple with both how we sound out loud (i.e., when we speak) and how we communicate in writing, on platforms that didn't exist even a few years ago. There is no right way to do this, only the right way for you and your goals.

Again, to focus on women for a beat: People (usually but not exclusively men) love to critique how women speak, especially younger women. After all, if one doesn't have a good argument counter to what someone is saying, simply attack how they sound when they're saying it. Whether it's the pitch of someone's voice, the upspeak at the end of their sentences, the vocal fry that echoes through a speech, or something else entirely, it is historically understood that Leaders Have Deep, Comforting, Solid Voices, and because women cannot access that range, we obviously cannot be leaders.

The worst example of this is obviously millennial Elizabeth Holmes of Theranos, who hilariously deepened her voice to try to leverage implicit beliefs around masculine credibility in order to fake her way through developing a medical device that didn't work, and ultimately conned patients and investors and landed herself in jail.

In much lower (and less illegal) stakes, next-gen leaders have been trying (and often failing) to adjust their presentations to meet the expectations of those around them. Flip the script: Once you become the leader, *you* are now defining what professionalism sounds like for your workplace—you get to decide.

Lisa of Gatheround told me about her first leadership job when she was in her mid-twenties—she simply wouldn't tell anyone her age. "I had to be really polished," she said. "I would wear makeup, and do my hair, and wear an outfit, and speak in a way that was articulate and thoughtful, and lower my voice."

She was so careful to behave the way she thought "grown-ups" acted. A few years later, in business school, one of her professors told her that acting that way made her "read as arrogant," which (1) was the first feedback she realized she could take seriously without taking literally and (2) helped her realize: "I had sort of faked it into not having to fake it anymore."

"I intentionally altered my leadership style and communication style to be a little bit more informal," she said. "I'm the CEO. I have the power. I have the authority." After spending years trying to fight to be taken seriously, she's won and subsequently is figuring out what her true style is without external pressures.

In a similar vein, Congresswoman Sara Jacobs, a millennial representing San Diego in the US House of Representatives, rolled her eyes as she told me that during her first campaign for office, "someone literally told me to wear a bikini so that men would want to vote for me."

After that race, she spent a lot of time thinking about how she sounded in debates. "You can hear my voice still upticks," she said, articulating the tendency she and so many women have to pitch up our sentences at the ends, even when we're not asking questions. Sara realized, sadly: "The men I was competing with weren't having to spend all that brainpower on what they sounded like."

Those dynamics are changing, albeit slowly. What's changing fast is how we communicate online.

So much of our performance of professionalism these days happens over Slack, text message, Signal groups, Zoom chats, or similar digital platforms. While postpandemic work and life are still in flux, it is clear that some iteration of remote work or hybrid work (meaning part in office, part from home) will stick around in many industries. And even in a fully in-office environment, we've got to deal with how we email, take calls, text our teams, and more.

This is where growing up online makes a difference. We have more venues to express ourselves and more inherent comfort in how to navigate them. If, for example, you got on AIM as a teenager and carefully set your away messages to best communicate a secret to your crush, have years-long Snapchat streaks with friends, or are a pro at picking which GIF to send to the group chat, you likely intuitively understand the subtleties of text- and image-based communications, even if you've never thought about how they apply to the workplace or your leadership persona.

Millennial tech entrepreneur and manager Steph Cheng grew up a gamer—digital communication is native to her. "You're always trying to display who you are but, in gaming, even more so because you're trying to imbue this character with a personality." She learned how to express both what she wants to say and how she feels, capturing the nuance necessary for communicating by memes, GIFs, emojis, and little side chats in Slack during a meeting.

She's got her finger on the pulse of what's appropriate for the chitchat spaces (conversations about the Olympics, or movies, or fun new recipes people are trying, as a few examples) and what needs to stay in one-on-one spaces or not in workspaces at all (like, say, a scene-by-scene breakdown of the one-night stand someone had the other night).

Emoji usage comes up a lot in conversations with next-gen leaders. A millennial working in tech told me about an experience at a former company where the CEO was conscientious to the point of paranoid about which emojis people might use on Slack when reacting to the news of layoffs—"Can we disable emoji reactions?" was literally a part of their communications-plan conversation as they worked through the steps.

Let me clear things up here: There is no such thing as the "professional" emoji. You have to make a judgment call for yourself about what you're trying to model for your team while also keeping in perspective: It's unlikely any boss you had before had to grapple with this question.

It's not just whether you should, for example, use the laughing-while-crying emoji, the skeleton emoji, or the coffin emoji when trying to indicate that something made you laugh. Every decision must be carefully examined. Consider the small but loud exclamation point!! It has become so cliché it's meme worthy to tell women to go through their email drafts and remove the exclamation points before they send.

In her excellent essay "A Theory of the Modern Exclamation Point," millennial Anne Helen Petersen describes the conversation around exclamation points as one really about tone and "the performance of niceness or seriousness."[1] Anne writes:

> The more marginalized your position (in society, in an industry) the more attention must be paid: one person told me she only occasionally uses an exclamation point when writing to friends, but would never, *ever* use one professionally. "I'm a Black woman," she simply explained.

Women in particular feel doomed if we use them too much and doomed if we don't use them enough. An email with exclamation points every third sentence screams our age and gender the same way using a period after "OK" or signing off text messages with a first name screams boomer. And yet, if we leave the !!s out, we are too serious, or too bitchy, or too insert-sexist-insult-here.

Another no-win communications category as norms have changed: profanity. This one is personal for me because, as you can probably tell, I swear a lot. The feedback I got most often about my first book (besides, you know, how helpful it was and how much it inspired people to run for office) was that I said "fuck" a lot.

Part of that was because I wrote from a place of genuine anger. Part of that was because in my nonwork life, I use profanity. But also, as part of the persona I've adopted for my work—which involves inspiring seemingly ordinary people to do extraordinary things such as run for office—I find profanity to be a useful tool to click in with my target demographic. This is one way I practice responsible authenticity: I try not to overdo it, but if something's fucked up, I call it fucked up.

I've modulated myself over the years, scaling back on my profanity as my anger has dissipated (or found new targets, more often)—but still, I'm acutely aware of how a curse word deployed strategically can turn a meh quote to a reporter into one that hits the lede of the story; how a strategic pause and then a "Well, everything they tell you is bullshit!" aside in a speech can bring the audience in on the joke with me.

Profanity can sharpen your argument, amp up your emotional stakes, or bring you down to make you seem more salt of the earth. It can also, with some audiences, and in some moments, distract from your goal. There are obviously complicated feelings around race, class, and gender and which people can use which words and in what way. (For example: A man using the word "bitch" comes off very differently than if I use it, even without any additional context.) Similarly, there is nuance across industries—profanity in a creative space might be totally appropriate while it'd get you fired from the classroom.

All these questions around emojis, exclamation points, and profanity are further compounded by the flattening of our communication channels. The tools we use to chat with our friends and the tools we use to communicate at work are one and the same. Everyone knows someone who knows someone with a horror story of sending a text to their boss that was meant for their romantic partner or best friend.

This flattening often leads to chaos. So many of the leaders I spoke with could point to a time when a team member—usually someone either younger who'd never been in an office before or someone older who didn't understand appropriate digital norms—used an internal-communications network in a way that was silly at best and wildly inappropriate or even illegal at worst. There's just so much room for error: When in doubt, save it for the group chat. And let's be precise: Your team Slack, your social media account, and your office LISTSERV are not the same as your group chat.

It's not just about style; it's also about substance. Especially in remote spaces, we have to balance wanting to get to know folks and seeming like a real person (because we are real people!) without overstepping or getting too loosey-goosey. Mazin Sidahmed, a millennial journalist and founder of *Documented*, a newsroom for and by immigrants in New York City, described the challenge he faced to get involved in the banter over Signal chats and engaging in the jokes, while knowing that his words carry greater weight when he participates. He's carved out the topics he can goof around on—specific sports teams, for example—and what he leaves for others to have as boss-free spaces.

He wants to joke around and participate in order to encourage others to participate and to emphasize that shooting the shit is important to build collegiality. But he can't do so at the expense of making someone feel unwelcome, nor at the expense of getting distracted from the work itself.

In the not-so-good-old days, this would have been solved in part by clear in-person signaling around what's appropriate when interacting with others—for example, a conversation in the break room or at the happy hour has a very different setting and tone than a conversation in a private office or a conference room. Now, there are fewer visual boundaries, which requires more leadership-defined ones and constant vigilance (and quick feedback) for those who cross them.

So when considering internal communication channels, professionalism, and how you participate, a few questions to ask and answer:

What's the most comfortable way for you to behave in an online social environment? Are you a quick and chatty DMer? Are you fluent with emojis? Do you find picking the right GIF to be deeply stressful because what if you pick the wrong one that gets you canceled? Be clear about what your actual preferences and style are here. Your best bet is to lean in to what feels natural, then dial it up or down from there.

Which topics are you most comfortable shooting the shit on? What do you have absolutely no interest in engaging with in a team space? Take your cues from Mazin and pick a few topics you can engage on in a meaningful way that feel comfortable to who you are. (For me, it's mostly books and the occasional Taylor Swift conversation as appropriate.) You don't have to be in every social space, but being carefully present helps remind people you're not just the boss; you're also a human.

What actually matters to you when it comes to informal communication? Whatever you land on, be intentional and follow through on it. For example: If you decide it's important to you to recognize people's birthdays, and you miss saying, "happy birthday [cake emoji]!!" to someone on Slack on their actual birthday, actively remind yourself to follow up with a belated message. Silly, maybe, but meaningful.

Consider the visuals you're presenting, especially when using video-chat technology. Your physical background doesn't need to be perfect, but it's an opportunity to subtly show a little bit of who you are. There are messy class divisions that can come up—the horror stories of people being let go by bosses Zooming in from their Martha's Vineyard vistas come to mind—so be intentional about the message your visuals set. There are real physical and financial constraints here, and I'm not going to dictate exactly what your background should look like, but like everything else, you should be intentional about what it looks like and understand it's sending a message the same way any photos or art you had up in your physical office might.

Once you understand the purpose behind the old-school rules of professionalism, consider how you can strategically break them to accomplish your goals. Use the exclamation points! Drop an emoji or curse word from time to time! Be a little silly when the moment is right! Just don't do it haphazardly.

It's not really about you. As long as you're furthering your goal, you're doing it right. You're the leader, so the way you sound and the way you speak *is* the way leaders sound and speak.

Tiana of the saving-democracy work has a tip for finding the courage to do it differently. She doesn't actually think of herself as brave. Rather, she treats decisions about her self-presentation as part of her job of "role modeling," opening the doors to other leaders to think expansively about what it means to show up and be in charge, in all the places and ways up-and-coming leaders need to be.

You're on the front lines of changing the definition of professionalism. Congrats and I'm sorry, in equal parts.

WHAT HAPPENS ON THE INTERNET RARELY STAYS ON THE INTERNET

How new generations relate to the internet is neatly summed up by this Bane quote from *The Dark Knight Rises*: "You merely adopted the dark. I was born in it."

Our comfort with the internet—and especially with social media—matters because the internet is a huge part of your persona as a leader. Your executive presence isn't just how you look, how you speak, or the way you can clearly present a forward-looking strategic plan with clear goals and tactics and measurable key performance indicators.

Your presence is also defined by what you post on your Instagram stories, which Facebook groups you might belong to (if you're on Facebook at all), and whether or not you're up-to-date on the latest TikToks or if you see them on Instagram reels a month later.

Leaders before us just don't live or exist on the internet in the same way. There's a 2018 congressional hearing that I think about approximately once a week. Facebook CEO Mark Zuckerberg was testifying before Congress about his company's privacy practices or lack thereof. Utah senator Orrin Hatch, eighty-four years old, asked Zuckerberg, "How do you sustain a business model in which users don't pay for your service?"

Zuckerberg's answer was a no duh for anyone who's ever used the platform and totally mind-blowing to the octogenarian senator: "Senator, we run ads."

If you've ever had to help your grandma set up her Wi-Fi or received a FWD:FWD:>> email from someone in your family or simply logged onto Nextdoor or a Facebook group in the last few years, you get it. The way (most) boomers use the internet is not a moral failing; they simply lack the fluency in the critical tools that will get us to the next era.

The ways next-gen leaders use the internet is part of what makes us different and, in many ways, makes our lives much harder: We get that the internet is a high-risk, high-reward strategic communications tool, and we're finding new ways to use it wisely. It's another way we build relationships with our teams—but as in any other context, those relationships are not on equal footing.

Like most millennials and nearly all Gen Zers, you've probably been online for more than half your life, even if your online habits have changed over the years. You've been using the internet broadly and social media specifically for fun, news, activism, shopping—it's not *separate* from your "real" life, it's just part of your life. (It could even be most of your life, depending on your personality, hobbies, and chosen career path.)

When you embrace a leadership role, your online presence, or lack thereof, takes on exponential importance. Your success is tied not just to what you do or say but how your team feels about what you do or say, the story they tell about it, and the proof points they attach to that story. You no longer have the luxury of posting without a care in the world.

If you're intentional and strategic, you can use the internet in ways that can exponentially further your leadership goals. If you're careless, you can truly fuck up your life (or, less dramatically, wildly undermine yourself). The boomer leaders who came before us didn't necessarily have to grapple with how to balance those risks and rewards. We do, and we don't have the freedom of starting with a fresh slate, which unfortunately too many guides to personal brand building assume.

In this chapter, we'll start with a look at parasocial relationships, which shape a core way we all interact with others on the internet and provide some insight into how our teams might be interacting with us.

Then we'll state the obvious: Trolls are everywhere. You'll meet two women online who've dealt with some real bullshit and stay online anyway, and learn their strategies for coping.

Then I'll give you what I'm affectionately framing as the honest girl's guide to personal social media branding that I couldn't ever really find in a leadership book: Namely, that it's both worth it and it super sucks. Then I offer a counterpoint, which is that logging off is good, as long as it's a choice.

Finally, some questions to consider as you evaluate how to be intentional about what you post, building off the earlier conversation on responsible authenticity. Whether you're extremely online or just a lurker, this chapter will leave you with an operating theory for your personal strategic communications both inside and outside of the workplace.

• • •

Let's start by defining our terms: A parasocial relationship is one between an individual (a follower) and a persona (real or fictional) they can't or don't actually know in real life but feel a deep connection with. The individual invests emotional energy in, spends time caring about, and is influenced by the persona. The persona may not know the individual exists.

Parasocial relationships have been part of the "discourse" in entertainment since the 1950s—someone can have a parasocial relationship with a celebrity, a newscaster, a politician, a musician, an athlete, a podcaster, whomever.

The relationship between leader and team is not a parasocial relationship by that strictest definition of the term. However, in the remote work environment especially, where casual relationship building is more controlled, it's not that far apart from the kind of parasocial relationship that exists between live streamers on Twitch or YouTube and their audiences, where it's what researchers call a "one-and-a-half way" relationship.[1]

Your team sees you on Zoom, in meetings, and on calls, and maybe follows you on social media. They know the responsibly authentic persona you're presenting, and they either professionally or personally (or both) may have invested energy in understanding you and your motivations because of the role you play in their livelihood.

So just as you think about what you wear, how you sound, and which emojis you use, you also have to think about your social media presence. The you they see on Zoom needs to match the you they follow online which needs to match the you they see in real-life gatherings—you need to have complete brand consistency.

I know, I know, you're not a brand—you're a person, with feelings and dignity and everything else that entails!

But given the way most people experience leaders in the modern workplace, you have to operate more intentionally. Depending on the scale of your leadership, there is likely space for reciprocity in some form or another, but it's never going to be quite as honest or as intimate as a real, one-on-one, vulnerable relationship. The power dynamics of your relationship have limits, a theme we'll come back to again and again.

You have to keep all that in mind when you're just scrolling your social media accounts over breakfast. As a leader, you don't necessarily have the luxury of tap-tap-tapping without consequence. Your presence in every possible space needs to reinforce the narrative you want to tell.

This came up most prominently in my conversation with millennial Tori Dunlap, who built her career online. She started with a blog about personal finance, which then became TikToks, which became a podcast that is consistently one of the top business podcasts in the world, a *New York Times* best-selling book, and a company, Her First $100K (HFK), with a dozen-plus employees that run an investment-education platform, programs to pay off debt, budgeting materials, career and negotiation support, and so much more.

Tori's been making videos and posting content through it all, while also running her company—she's both the wizard behind the curtain as well as the talent in front of it. She has over five million followers across her platforms and describes herself as having the "teeny tiny, just the tiniest bit of lowercase-*f* fame," and even that is sometimes too much.

Her comments are a mix of positive—people thanking her for her financial-literacy content, describing the ways she's helped them get out of debt, save money, and seek new paths for themselves—and some of the most toxic bullshit you can imagine, especially from men shit talking her appearance. "Imagine walking down the street past one hundred people, and they're all saying something to you, and maybe ninety-five of them are lovely, but five of them are awful. It's still overwhelming. It's still crazy," she said, reflecting on the stream of feedback from the internet.

That makes it really hard and also really necessary to have boundaries about what she puts on the internet and what she shares with her team. It's not that the online version of Tori isn't real, but it's a very specific version of her. "I aspire to be as unbothered as [the public version of me] is," she said, laughing. But like her red lipstick and leather jacket, it's part of a performance.

Her followers—and her staff, to a certain extent—have expectations of her that she simply can't meet. People who follow her think they know her based off of her content and then get mad when she "makes some sort of decision that doesn't align with the version of me they had in their head." I heard echoes of this throughout my conversations with leaders who had one one-hundredth the size of Tori's social media following: something along the lines of "my employees get mad when I don't meet their expectations, even though those expectations were not based on reality."

Tori—and many others I talked to of varying social media exposures—brought up the anxiety of knowing any Zoom meeting could be recorded, any email could be screenshotted, any post online could be taken out of context. There is no room for turning it off, even in the highest-trust environments. The balance between internal management and external communication is exhausting and requires constant context shifting and a perpetual balancing act between different personas.

Part of the solution is to show vulnerability and our more human sides. But as I've been hammering home: You can't *really* do that, at least not to the fullest extent possible. Your team will always have a relationship with you that is a little closer to parasocial than not.

If you feel that distance, and feel like they're telling a story about you that is separate from who you are, that's not because you're necessarily doing something wrong. It's baked into the power dynamics.

Congresswoman Alexandria Ocasio-Cortez (AOC) beat out a Democratic incumbent in New York City in a 2018 primary and became the youngest woman to ever serve in Congress when she took office at twenty-nine years old. A former waitress and organizer turned elected official, she's raised the bar on how to use social media in a way that feels authentic, genuine, and strategic, and for leaders looking to strike a balance online, she's at the top of the list of excellence.

The tools and tactics have shifted over the years, but even looking back, she was always on her A game online. From a compelling video that could help her raise money to visual branding that stood out among the crowd to content that was real (but with boundaries!)—AOC seemed like an authentic version of herself online because, like any millennial, she'd grown up online and felt comfortable using the internet to express herself.

In particular, she's strategically used live streams to connect to her base: From logging on to Twitch to play video games—which she described to *The Washington Post* as "kind of like the way some of my colleagues talk about golf"—to using Instagram Live to talk directly to the camera about what she experienced during the January 6 insurrection, she's cultivated a remarkable amount of intimacy with her community. I remember that 2021 stream in particular, sitting in my bedroom, riveted to my phone as she looked into the camera and expressed the panic she felt hiding behind her office door. It was like FaceTiming with my friend, who just happened to be the congresswoman from New York. (To be clear: She's not my friend; we've never met.)

Going through the screenshots on my phone, it seems like every few months I have one from one of AOC's Instagram stories—whether because I laughed when she described the Capitol building as a kind of Hogwarts, I found it compelling when she was explaining how she chose a dress to wear to a diplomatic meeting, or I wanted her recommendation on which BB cream to use as foundation, her social media has stuck with me.

AOC has made the highfalutin office of United States representative seem approachable and real and given us, her followers, a carefully curated feeling of community and insider-ness with her. She isn't a stranger or an elite—she is one of us, while also leading us. I trust her because, thanks to her social media, I feel like I know her.

I also know that I absolutely don't know her, not even a little. Instagram is not reality, and as a member of Congress, she is actually one of the more powerful people in the country. I only know the version of her she presents online, and I can tell exactly how careful she is about it. That's a model for us all.

• • •

I'm going to state the obvious here: Social media can be a necessary and positive tool for advancement—it can win elections, change lives, and transform societies. It can also, on a personal level, totally mess with your head unless you set clear and explicit boundaries. Your followers, whether it's online or your team in real life, don't really know you, even when they think they know you. The dynamics of a semiparasocial relationship are inherently uneven. So when you get trolled, which given any amount of public exposure, you probably will, you need to be firm in your sense of self.

Tiara Mack, a Gen Z Black lesbian Southerner, moved to Rhode Island for college and stayed after graduation. She decided to run for office to take on an incumbent in her own party who refused to support abortion access. Tiara declared from day one of her ultimately victorious campaign, "I'm going to be unapologetically Black, I'm going to be unapologetically queer, and I'm going to be unapologetically young, and I'm going to push back against the system that tells us we don't deserve justice now."

Tiara had always been on social media, mostly with little consequence. That changed on July 4, 2022, when she posted an eight-second clip of her in a yellow bikini, upside down in a headstand, twerking on the beach, ending with a smile and asking viewers to "Vote Senator Mack" leading up to her reelection. The quick clip went viral, racking up hundreds of thousands of views.

Shit hit the fan. The Rhode Island Republican Party used screenshots of the video to fundraise. Tucker Carlson played it on his nightly show on Fox News, mocking her. Republican representative Marjorie Taylor Greene, the notorious troll from Georgia, viciously insulted her. Tiara got a wave of death threats and racist and sexist harassment over every possible channel.

Tiara told local news a few days after:

> It's been wild. I have seen and heard it all. I have a 9-to-5 job that I've been going to daily. I've also been canvassing my neighbors, and I've been able to talk to many of my voters. I watched a 10-month-old baby last night. So my life has been going on as normal. But this idea of Tiara Mack, meme sensation, I guess, has, like, really blown up. . . .
>
> [The internet] is about creating a separate persona in some respects, but still being able to say, I want people to

> see at least some part of me in them. I want the next generation of leaders to see that they can lead an authentic life and draw people into their message, into their platforms. *It's about showing the imperfections when you need to. It's about showing the failures when you need to, and then also having fun when you need to.*

That emphasis is mine—social media is strategic: showing the imperfections, the failures, and the fun *when you need to* and when it serves your goals.

Tiara faced harassment going into the next month and beyond. But fuck 'em. Tiara handily won reelection. As she explained to me, "The folks that were meant to get it got it, and the folks that didn't get it are the folks that were never meant to get it." The pearl-clutching racists may not have liked her TikToks, but the young people who showed up at the polls sure did.

What Tiara went through was on the more extreme end of what many, many people, but especially women, people of color, or LGBTQ+ people, experience on the internet: The haters and trolls are everywhere and have only gotten worse.

Leadership means taking a stand, and taking a stand means some people are going to disagree with you. When that disagreement shows up online, it can quickly get personal, because online, you're not a real person—as Tiara put it, you're just an abstraction. Even knowing that, being on the receiving end of nastiness and cruelty can be exhausting (or worse) and can quickly get dangerous.

Tiara's story illustrates one important takeaway for you to consider with your own social media presence: If your leadership takes you into a more public role, your trolls may grow in volume, and it may feel more personal. *It's not personal, even when the comments specifically say: This is personal! It's still not.* They're mad about what you represent: change, disruption, a force against the status quo. That depersonalization doesn't make them go away, but it can turn down the impact on your sense of self.

Another example to consider as you think about your social media presence—but fair warning, this one gets sad. Millennial Ashley Spivey, a *Bachelor* contestant turned nanny turned influencer, has built a community that trusts her because they feel like they know her (even when she'll fully admit: They don't!). Her online presence and her leadership style are vulnerable, accessible, and fully on the level.

Over her first eight years with a substantial following on social media, Ashley's content across Twitter, Snapchat, and then later primarily Instagram was the ephemera of her life: a mix of politics, pictures of the boy she nannied (with the parents' permission, of course), her workouts, her skin-care routine, thoughts on *The Bachelor* (a topic that faded out later on as the series refused to grapple with its issues around race and consent), and especially the books she was reading.

Her online story evolved in 2019. As the possibility of an abortion ban became more likely, Ashley and her husband were going through their own fertility journey. She'd recently had a miscarriage and, subsequently, an abortion to complete the procedure.

Instead of staying silent about it, Ashley posted a gut-wrenching series of images, sharing how it felt to sit in the room with her husband and sister, looking at the sonogram of an embryo that had stopped growing. She was directly connecting the dots for her followers—the black-and-white image on that screen and the D&C procedure she had after was exactly what antiabortion legislators were fighting about.

"I thought it was important to start having these conversations," she said to me. "People were thinking about all the ways that women's reproductive rights could be affected beyond abortion. I really didn't want to hide it."

She continued to post through her fertility challenges, sharing through Instagram stories as she underwent more treatments, had more miscarriages, and grieved along the way. In 2020, she got pregnant with a little boy just as the pandemic began, and her followers celebrated with her. Over the course of her pregnancy, her stories were peppered with baby-gear purchases, Q&As about her pregnancy workouts and skin-care-routine modifications, and her excitement for long-awaited motherhood. Her followers were so excited to see the person they'd come to know, care for, and respect be so happy.

In November 2020, we mourned with her when her son, CJ, was stillborn.

What happened to Ashley next makes me so angry I want to scream on her behalf each time I think about it: In the weeks and months after she had to deliver her dead child, her account was swarmed by anti-vaxxers blaming her for her son's death. Nearly all the comments are gone now, thank goodness, but I remember seeing them in real time. Some were probably bots, but many were real people who felt it was acceptable to be personally cruel to a woman in mourning.

She and her followers fought back, reporting them to Instagram, calling them out when possible, and drawing attention especially to the hypocrites in her DMs. Like Tiara, Ashley couldn't escape the haters. She could only set her own boundaries and decide how to react.

If you ask me, she would have been fully within her rights to log off, throw her phone into the river, and never reemerge onto the internet. Instead, she kept sharing, letting people in on how she coped with this loss, showing us the memorial bench she set up for CJ, and thanking followers for the hundreds of small gifts and letters she received—people who'd experienced similar losses would DM her with deep gratitude for her openness.

In early 2022, Ashley shared her next attempt at IVF, celebrating her pregnancy with her community. And once again, we were brought with her to her loss. She posted through another miscarriage—literally, she put up a picture of her blood-soaked jeans to her stories, with captions on how it felt and how she knew something was wrong. This time, Ashley made headlines, representing a shift in the discourse toward more public conversations about reproductive health and pregnancy loss.

When she got pregnant with her daughter in March 2022 through another IVF procedure, she highlighted the unique experience of pregnancy after loss and shared her anxieties. She set boundaries around when she wanted advice and when she just wanted to share and didn't hesitate to block people who crossed the line.

Through it all, Ashley also kept posting the fun stuff—book reviews, skin care, cooking, political stories, and her little dog, Jackson. When her daughter, Penny, was born alive and perfect, it was like all her followers could exhale. These days, her feed is all of the above, plus the trials and tribulations (and incredible joys!) of early motherhood. And yet, there are still things she keeps offline—her husband's work, her extended social circle, the personal details (including the last name of) the family she nannied for, among other things—as she is acutely aware of what is and is *not* the focus of her content.

What has become a prominent feature in her content is targeted activism, especially in pushing for paid leave after pregnancy loss, which was spurred after receiving a DM from a follower who told Ashley how hard it was to get leave from work after her own miscarriage. Ashley started encouraging her followers to have conversations with their own HR departments about new policies.

She shared success stories, gave scripts, and created space for commiseration through her account. Dozens of companies now have this policy, in no small part because of Ashley.

Unlike many people professionally online, Ashley is aggressively transparent about the machinations of being an influencer—she says she's always thought too many influencers were "scammy"—so when she runs advertising, she tells her followers the metrics she's being paid on so they know the best way to help her. When she asks her followers to donate to a charity, she shows the receipt from her donation, too.

Her social media account is not just a place she talks about her leadership—it *is* where she leads, brand deals and all. She sets the tone for what she expects of the community she's built across her comments and her Instagram DMs (of which she gets more than six hundred a day and tries to answer them all!) and puts enough of herself out there that they can trust her.

I asked her if she felt a responsibility to her followers. She paused for a good ten seconds, considering the question, then said, "I do. We're in it together. I feel like I can't let them down, and I don't want to let them down."

Two big takeaways for you to consider from Ashley's and Tiara's styles of social media usage:

First: If it ever reaches a point that you do not want to have to deal with, you can and should protect your peace. Log off. Make your accounts private. Hand off your passwords to someone else or shut the accounts down entirely. No leadership goal is worth the hit to your mental health.

Second, and I say this because sometimes the haters will defend themselves as if they're good-faith critics: Trolling and doxing are different from feedback.

Feedback is a gift that, when delivered thoughtfully with compassion, clarity, and integrity, can make you better. You will never be doing everything right, you always have opportunities for growth, and there *are* people who you can and should trust to give you honest constructive guidance. Online trolls, especially ones who do not actually know you, are *not* those people. They're just assholes.

Even if your leadership role is not explicitly public, you still might encounter some online trolling that eats away at you. Maybe former employees will shit talk you on social media—a deeply nonstrategic move on their part, but hey, everyone has their own goals—or maybe your company or brand ends up on the receiving end of a lot of online hate. Whatever it may be: They have a right to say whatever they want, and you have a right to mute or ignore it at your leisure. I say this only kind of joking: What other people have to say or post about you online is none of your business.

The dynamics are slightly different when it comes to what your team says about you, whether you hear it firsthand or third, but I find it useful to remind myself: They only know as much about me as I tell them. The relationship is not even. It's not fully on the level. It never can be. I take my team's negative feedback more seriously than I do the trolls' on the internet, for sure—but I also take it with a certain amount of depersonalization. Critiquing the work is one thing; critiquing the person is another.

• • •

For most next-gen leaders, me included, it's a no-brainer to think about our leadership online as part of our power—a vast majority of the folks I talked to had some kind of internet presence. Whether that's causation (being aggressively present online directly helps you succeed) or correlation (the people who tend to obtain some kind of power in this stage of life are also the kind of people who post a lot) is not worth detangling too much.

For most people, though, being online is about consumption, not production. In 2023, Pew Research Center found that on TikTok, the top 25 percent of users produced 98 percent of all content—so in all likelihood, you're probably a lurker with the occasional double tap or "happy birthday!!" comment now and again.

If that's you, I respect it. But as with all the communication tools we've discussed so far, I want to make it clear: If you're a leader, logging off is as much a choice as being online. You should know what you're leaving on the table in either scenario.

So even though I hate both-sides-ism, I want to talk through the options.

OPTION 1:
Be a poster.

As I said, I am professionally and personally online, both in addition to and as part of my job. It's fun (sometimes), it helps our goals (usually), it sucks (for my sanity)—all three are true at the same time.

When we started Run for Something back in 2017, I did not expect social media to be such a prominent part of my work. I had maybe a few thousand followers on Twitter (or X, or whatever we're calling it these days), and my Instagram feed was mostly pictures of my dog, plus a few graphics urging people to vote. I treated the whole thing like it was me talking to my friends because that's mostly what it was.

The day we launched, the organization wasn't more than a legal entity, a plan on Medium, and a website I shared on every platform I was on. Over the first few months, I live-posted my way through building the company, sharing how much money we raised and how many candidates had signed up and occasionally snarked on political topics that were relevant to the organization's mission.

Social media—both my personal accounts and the brand's accounts, which were also often run by me—was how the organization stayed afloat. Twitter threads would raise tens of thousands of dollars; one viral post could reach hundreds of potential candidates for office. I knew how to work the algorithm to find the right balance of action, information, and entertainment.

I was thoughtful about what I posted, often gut checking with my cofounder if I thought what I was going to say would hurt our carefully crafted reputation. Our brand was positivity, optimism, and a focus on local politics—which meant I had to be mostly positive and optimistic (which I genuinely am!).

As my audience grew from a few thousand to tens of thousands and I was regularly getting shared by accounts with hundreds of thousands or even millions of followers, I had to be more intentional. One wrong post could damage our credibility, lose my organization key funding streams, or upset the wrong political partner.

I mixed it up, bouncing between news stories about our candidates, baseball tweets (I was an intense Washington Nationals fan until they won the World Series in 2019, which is the last season that counted in my heart), and the occasional personal-but-not-that-personal anecdote, all with asks for people to further our cause. It took an immense amount of effort, and I could never truly log off, but it worked.

That's not to say I did everything right—I've been smack-dab in the center of a few shitstorms over the years. A poorly phrased social media post I dashed off while reading the news on the subway made me a main character on the internet for the day, as my notifications kept ding-ding-dinging with people piling on to make sure I knew that they had interpreted what I'd said as problematic. I felt bad, not just because I had said something others had deemed hurtful but because my sloppiness reflected poorly on my organization.

Other times, the shitstorm is just mean. A video I did for an online media outlet did pretty well on Facebook, reaching hundreds of thousands of viewers. Like an absolute idiot, I was curious what viewers had to say about it so I skimmed through the comments. Seeing even a few "fat bitch"–type remarks left me stinging. I found it useful to reframe it: If my online presence is reaching enough people to get trolled, then I'm reaching outside my echo chamber to people who may disagree with me. For my purposes, that's mostly a good sign.

As the years have gone by, our staff and budgets have grown, and the pressure has gotten more intense. I know members of my team follow me on every platform, so I have to be thoughtful of not just what I'm posting or how I'm amplifying our work but even about what time I'm doing it—if I share something online in the middle of a meeting I'm sitting in with some of our team members, they'll know I'm multitasking.

I have to comment on our candidates' posts with positivity and celebrate their wins. I have to compliment our partners online because saying nice things costs me nothing and gets us all goodwill. I have to double tap when one of our staff members shares something exciting going on for them—not just because I want to (and I do! I always do!) but because it's a good and easy way to support them as full people. It is in and of itself a full-time job on top of my already full-time job.

I wonder how other executives have time for this. How do they balance all-day meetings and events with staying up-to-date on social media, making videos, or flipping through Instagram stories?

The answer is simple. Many of the leaders who came before either don't have social media in the same way or don't do it themselves. They don't have to think about their TikTok presence because it'd be crazy for them to be on TikTok; no one is expecting them to be engaging in an Instagram Live stream in anything other than a carefully produced marketing-team production.

That's not the case for so many of the next-gen leaders I talk to—we are expected to be ourselves on the internet, on top of everything else on our to-do lists.

Social media has been a double-edged sword for me and for so many of the people I talked to. Much like Tori Dunlap's company, Run for Something likely would not exist in its current state—and, if we're being honest with each other, I would probably not be writing this book—without social media.

It is often fun, structurally addicting, and in the biggest news moments, fully necessary to understand what's happening and help shape the discourse in ways that keep my work relevant. I am proud of the intentionality I've brought to my social media presence and the way it's furthered my goals.

But, without a doubt, it also sucks for my mental health. I've experienced the self-loathing spiral that comes when a post gets picked up by an account interpreting it in bad faith that leads to a barrage of comments critiquing not my work but me personally. (I mostly mute that stuff because again: It's none of my business what people have to say about me online. But still, it sucks!) I've set clear boundaries about pictures of my kids online because, while I can mostly take the criticism and haters, my perfect daughters should never be targets.

And when social media is inherently tied to work, there is no distinction between posting for work and posting for fun. I can't ever fully unplug. Vacation means deleting the apps from my phone, which eventually helps but also reveals just how deep the muscle memory runs each of the first one hundred times I unlock my phone and unintentionally tap over to where the apps usually live on my home screen, only to find myself opening whatever app has replaced it instead.

Ultimately, the bits and pieces of my life that I regularly share online have become part of my brand. I pick and choose carefully: things like my very poorly behaved (but very photogenic!) dog, occasional Playbills from shows we see or fun NYC adventures, and of course, news stories about or related to Run for Something.

Most consistently, I regularly post reviews of the hundreds of books I read a year—sometimes serious literature, but more often spicy romance novels, rated on a one-to-four chili pepper scale. A more prudish boomer might suggest it's inappropriate for a serious political strategist and nonprofit executive to post an Instagram review of a four-chili-pepper novel with extremely dirty sex scenes. That suggestion would be wrong for two reasons: (1) Those kinds of posts help show people I'm a full, real human who both loves my job and is more than my job, and (2) romance novels rule.

It's taken me years of practice and a lot of mistakes, but the place I've landed, and that I hope you'll land by the end of this chapter, is that social media is not just for fun or for online-shopping recs—it's a strategic communications tool just like a memo or a PowerPoint slide deck.

The sillier topics I post about online are the same ones I choose to chat about with my staff; the serious topics I share about are the same things I want to bring up with stakeholders like donors, the press, or our political partners.

It's all intentional and goal oriented. If you decide to be online, that's the whole damn point.

OPTION 2:
Log off.

There are certainly some leadership roles or sectors where being loud online is almost all risk and minimal reward—take education as just one example. Every few weeks, it feels like there's a news story about a teacher getting fired for posting something online. Hell, I talked with one high school teacher in the Midwest who was on the receiving end of a parent complaint simply for liking one controversial celebrity's Instagram post.

While some teachers have used social media to successfully raise money for their classrooms through crowdfunding campaigns or make some side cash themselves, most keep their shit locked down. They know that as leaders in the community and important figures in families' lives, they are targets for a parent looking at someone to be mad at or a student looking to find some hot goss.

You also might decide that, as you grow in leadership, you want to scale back your online presence or that, in your particular circumstance, lurking is the ultimate power move. Maybe you just don't feel comfortable living your life in public; you don't want to share pics of your family, or post links to news stories you find interesting, or feel compelled to issue a statement on every breaking news story. That's okay! You don't have to, and you aren't unusual in making that choice. As many social media companies have become more unambiguously evil (and the news environment generally became more exhausting) logging off is becoming more and more common. Analog is cool again! You do what you've got to do. Just be intentional about it.

OPTION 3:
Target your communications.

There's also a middle ground of sorts. Millennial Alida Garcia, a leading strategist in progressive politics, has a fully private Instagram account—mostly to keep her kids off the public internet—but she's constantly thinking about what she's posting. "I lovingly call myself an influencer of influencers in this policy space," she said, "but I'm not trying to speak at scale." She knows who her friends and followers are and knows that she can influence them through what she shares online.

Alida's work over the last decade has intentionally required her to put aside her own voice at times—she literally writes and develops public-advocacy campaigns for presidents, senators, celebrities, and other public figures. There's a downside to this for her career, she acknowledged: "Oftentimes people equate visibility to work, and visibility to them is 'Have I seen that in your Instagram stories?' Sometimes, it's not strategic for you to be the one posting; sometimes the intention is for someone else to post because of your actual message and audience goals. But when you're not creating a visible narrative about you and your work in this era, it can feel like maybe you're undercutting yourself."

Social media is by definition performative—but that performance matters. The public or semipublic square of the internet is where you can shape what others think about your work. If you're not giving others a narrative of your own creation, they're going to fill in the blanks themselves. If nothing else: Consider your social media an extension of your résumé because it is almost 100 percent likely that next time you apply for a job, someone with decision-making power will take a look at what you've posted. What do you want them to see?

Alida's limited presence online is an explicit and intentional choice. "It's a constant tug and pull for me," she said. For now, she's telling her story to a strategic audience. If you decide to go one step further and lurk or log off entirely, that's a choice, too.

* * *

Your leadership role might not be as pronounced as a member of Congress's. You might not be trying to win votes or get press or reach hundreds of thousands of people (at least, not yet).

But just like everything else at work, you need to be intentional about your online communication. The internet is where you have perhaps the most control over how your story gets told—it's where you can most directly shape your personal brand.

I know you may be eye rolling here because thinking about your personal brand can feel gross. But as a leader, your role is to unite others around your shared vision for the future, whether that's the future of your community, your company, or your parents' neighborhood group chat. I'll keep repeating this because it's annoyingly true: How people feel about you is as important (and arguably more important) as how they feel about your ideas.

First, revisit that personal narrative you considered earlier. That's the core of who you are—that's the meat of your personal brand and a clear starting point.

Your next step is to do a self-audit. Make a list or spreadsheet of everywhere you show up online—consider every social media platform you're on or have ever been on and any websites you regularly comment on and do a quick online search on yourself. (While you're at it, set up a news alert for your name—it may feel weird, but it's worth knowing if you're showing up on the internet somewhere!)

Take a look through each profile and all your posts or content with fresh eyes: Which key words would you use to describe your online persona? Which topics do you seem to talk about a lot? What kinds of images do you post? Do you treat one platform differently from another? If a stranger just happened across something you posted, or a few things you posted, what would they take away?

This is not the time for judgment—despite what content marketers might tell you, there is no singularly correct way to use social media. Instead, think of social media usage along the spectrum of "intentional" to "haphazard."

You can use it with thoughtfulness, applying a goal-oriented approach to your online presence, understanding that all communication is strategic communication—or you can treat the internet like your group chat and just toss stuff out into the world without thinking twice.

Since you've likely been posting or sharing stuff online for the better part of a decade, you may have a lot to go through. As you pull together your list, take a moment to peek at your privacy settings and see what kind of access others may have. Some platforms also have tools that let you see what you posted on that day years ago—that's an easy way to clean up your archives over time if there's a chance you shared something in the past that present-day you might not be so proud of. (You can also just nuke your entire posting history if that strikes your fancy!)

At this point, you should have a good sense of where you are, what kind of person you present as, and what raw materials you're working with. You know who you are, who your persona needs to be, and where your boundaries need to be strongest.

A few more questions to consider as you shape your strategy:

What are you trying to accomplish online? You could hope to further awareness for your company or highlight your achievements so a potential employer thinks you're a good hire, or so your new C-suite peers take you seriously. Your goals could also be something specific and tangible like "Raise X dollars" or "Bring in three new clients this quarter."

Does your team see your online presence? I don't need to know them or know the details of your circumstances to know that the answer is always yes, and you should operate under the assumption that the answer is always yes. Even if you think you're as under the radar as possible, even if all your accounts are locked down and you've approved every single follower one by one, your team is seeing your online presence. You may dispute me on this. Trust me—they do, especially if they think you don't want them to. The curious ones will look you up online and the committed ones will find you. This was mostly a rhetorical question because you have to operate assuming they will see everything!

What kind of content do you need to put out in the world to achieve your goal, and where do you need to share it? This is a tactical question: Which platforms further your goal—where are the people you need to reach? Are you going all in on LinkedIn, or do you need a newsletter? Maybe your best use of time is making videos, or maybe it's some other type of content that doesn't exist as of this writing but is all of a sudden really popular. Maybe it's a niche social media community. Where do you need to be, and what kind of stuff works there?

The key here is not to force it. If you know you're never going to be comfortable making videos with your face front and center, don't. If you're not comfortable with graphic design (and have no interest in getting comfortable with graphic design), don't try to fake it. While there is no one right way to use social media, there is definitely a wrong way.

Reverse the question: What kind of content and which platforms would undermine your goals? If your goal is "Be taken seriously by my new direct reports," then flooding your social media accounts with silly goofy memes might not be the best way to go about that. (Unless your job is in making silly goofy memes, then maybe it is!)

If you feel that gut instinct to ask whether something is okay to post, it's probably best to assume the answer is no. Maybe it'd be okay—maybe you're being overly cautious or hesitating out of fear. Only you can know your boundaries and what would ultimately do more harm than good. But the more you develop the scaffolding of your strategic online persona, the more your gut will tell you when you're not being true to that framework. When in doubt, at the very least, take a beat and think through it a little more. If you're going to invite the shitstorm, do it intentionally.

How do you want your team to behave online? How you act creates the permission structure for how your team should act. If you don't want them sharing a particular type of content, or posting through meetings, or lifting up news stories that might undermine your org's mission, you shouldn't, either. While it may not be appropriate for you to set formal social media policies for your team, you can model good behavior.

Finally, I again want to give you permission to log off or, at the very least, take a step back if using social media in this way doesn't feel authentic to you.

This may seem hypocritical given what I wrote earlier, but if you don't think your goals can be furthered by your social media, or if you're comfortable with where you're at, you don't have to be as online as most of the leaders laid out in this chapter. You can lock everything down, update your LinkedIn page once in a while, and call it a day. As I like to say to political candidates when something irrelevant or unhelpful comes up in the news cycle they're overly eager to comment on: Shutting the fuck up is always an option available to you.

The internet is a strategic communications tool—use it strategically.

PART TWO

If the questions include . . .

How do you create a workplace where people can be their real selves but don't have to be their full selves?

How do you lead in a remote work environment?

Is work-life balance (or work-life integration) even possible?

How do I satisfy changing demands for transparency?

The answer is:

Through extreme (and well-documented!) clarity on who you are as an organization, what kind of behavior you will encourage, and what kind of behavior you as a leader model.

PEOPLE SHOULD BE THEIR REAL SELVES, NOT THEIR FULL SELVES

In part one, we talked about how you present yourself as a leader. In part two, we're switching gears because leadership isn't *actually* about you—it's about your team and what they're able to accomplish when you set them up to succeed.

And just as it's become very fashionable in the last few years for leaders to bring more humanity and vulnerability to work with them, it's similarly come in vogue to implore all people to "bring your full self to work."

Like much of next-gen leadership, this ethos is in direct conversation with the traditional boomer style of an explicit distinction between work and life—between the hours of nine and five, you're not a real person, you're a worker. This made sense, especially when many jobs were primarily routine tasks that didn't allow for pretense about some bigger ideal. The ethos was also (at least, in some cases) meant to promote inclusivity and diversity in the workplace, albeit with mixed results.

In the last decade, the vibes have gone full on in the other direction: Work is for everything!

As other institutions have crumbled (see: headlines about the demise of religion, civic clubs, volunteerism, third spaces, and basically every other trend piece in *The Atlantic* over the last five years), work has expanded to take up the room left behind, particularly for those with college degrees.[1] The Pew Research Center asked Americans what gives their life meaning, and respondents were nearly twice as likely to name their career as their spouse. (Bleak!)

In some ways, this makes a ton of sense: We spend forty-plus hours a week at work. Many people meet their partners or best friends at work and derive some or most of their day-to-day social lives from professional spaces.[2] During the early days of the pandemic, for those who weren't laid off, work was the only routine we could structure our days around.

In the current partial or fully work-from-home era, our virtual office can bleed into our home life and blur the boundaries. Who we are and what we do have become interchangeable for so many of us, pushing us to expect all of our fulfillment to come from our jobs and to bring our full selves to our job in order to seek that fulfillment.

But the connective theses of (1) "work must be our whole identity" and (2) "we must bring our whole identities to work" are individually and collectively broken. Work can't be everything we are, and we can't bring our full selves to work. It's simply not set up for that.

In part one, I made the argument for being clear and intentional about who you are as a leader, what your boundaries are, and what you're communicating as a person—both for your benefit and for your team's. Over the next three sections, I'll lay out exactly why it's imperative for you to do the same thing for the organization. Get ready because, instead of topics like fashion choices and emoji usage, we're getting into things like HR policies, workplace culture, equity and inclusivity, work-rest integration, and expectations around transparency. While these particulars might not perfectly map on to your leadership space (especially if it's outside of work), and while you may not have the power to implement everything in these sections, consider what you can translate over.

I feel particularly passionate about this based on my decade in politics, where the expectation is not just that you give your work everything you've got (time, energy, physical and mental health, etc.) but that you do it while spilling your guts to your colleagues.

It's literally a tactic trained into many of the folks in my industry—we're encouraged to metaphorically bleed using a skill defined by Marshall Ganz as "story of self," which asks leaders to show "why you have been called to what you have been called to," as a way of weaving a narrative that connects who you are to who the community is and tying that all together with the urgency of the moment. (Said another way: Tell the people why you do this work.)

In expert hands, this process is a powerful way of inspiring people to take action. In what I'll generously call *less-expert hands*, a story-of-self exercise often becomes a trauma Olympics, as people (consciously or not) compete to see who has the most credibility to do the work and claim the mantle of leadership.

I struggle whenever asked for a story of self because the boring but truthful answer is I do this work because I believe it matters, end of story. There was no traumatic experience, no personal breaking point that led me to politics. I just wanted—and still want—to make the world better. I think politics is a critical (if sometimes slow or disappointing) way of accomplishing that, and I find it all interesting and well suited to my skills.

So I have a tough time in some of the group settings I am professionally obligated to be in, especially those that begin with story of self. As I sit and listen to others tell of devastating experiences—homelessness, death and illness, assault and abuse—I ache for them, and at the same time, I question whether professional colleagues are necessarily the best audience for this pain.

As the years have gone by, I've had more and more experiences that validate this boundary for me. The breaking point was in June 2022. I was four months pregnant with my first daughter and had just gotten over the worst part of the nausea, only to enter the superfun phase of that pregnancy where my tailbone hurt whenever I sat on hard surfaces. I was not particularly pumped to be flying three hours then driving another two to attend a retreat in the mountains, but it was all convened by a major funder, so I couldn't really say no. The guiding language on the agenda implored us to be ready to bring our full, most authentic selves to the gathering space and to be prepared for vulnerability.

We opened with a sharing circle, for which we'd been asked to prepare by bringing an object that illustrated why we do this work. It would be neither the first nor the last time I'd use my kids for a story—I held out a Run for Something baby onesie (always on-brand!) to explain that while I started out doing this work to satisfy my own interests, I now do it to create a better world for my future offspring.

In a week where we were expecting the Supreme Court decision overturning *Roe v. Wade*, I was urgently aware of what it meant to be bringing a daughter into the world in this moment, in this country, and what I could to do make things better for her.

It was personal, sure, but a level of personal I could handle—it was responsible authenticity, giving just enough away without crossing the boundaries I set for myself.

The retreat continued to get more touchy-feely and uncomfortable. There were walking meditations, more sessions imploring us to lay our personal traumas out for the group to chew on, and evening social activities that were intended to foster interpersonal relationships but left me, a pregnant woman—who, even when not pregnant, doesn't drink heavily or do drugs and especially doesn't partake in substances at work events—feeling isolated.

The last day of the retreat was the day the Supreme Court decision in the abortion case came down, bright and early over breakfast. I viscerally remember: The sun was shining, the birds were chirping, and by the time I'd finished my scrambled eggs, my tiny fetus had more rights in utero than she would the moment she was born. I had a tough time keeping it together for the concluding sessions and stepped away, closing out a rough week.

A few weeks after the event, I got a call from the organizer who told me in no uncertain terms that my bad attitude about the experience had ruined it for everyone. They critiqued my tone, my composure, and my entire approach to the event. (I later asked around to other attendees because, if I had in some way affected others' experiences, I of course wanted to apologize—alas, no one could validate that.)

Regardless, if nothing else, I had seriously offended the organizer of the event. That was bad! I shouldn't have done that, both because they'd generously hosted me and because they're a generous supporter of the work I live and breathe. I apologized profusely, both on the phone and in writing, and proceeded to be on my absolute best behavior.

But I've been reflecting on that experience in the time since and have concluded that multiple things can be true: While I absolutely should have put on a better professional face because that's my job, I also reject the premise of the setting entirely.

Being asked to unload my personal trauma, lean into the openness of meditation, or get shit-faced with my colleagues is not appropriate for every environment, especially one in which the power dynamics are wildly uneven. I was asked to be vulnerable without any thought of the consequences of that request.

The leader of that event set me up to fail. I've carried that experience with me since, affirmed in the belief that we do our teams a disservice by asking people to bring parts of themselves to work that work is ill-suited to handle.

The solution for this—creating space for people to be their real selves but not their full selves—is to literally tell our teams what they can expect from work, what work expects from them, and what success or failure looks like, both in work product and in behavior.

Forget what you know about "show, don't tell." In this case, it's show *and* tell, and then tell again, and tell them a third (and fourth, and fifth) time, and codify it into policies.

It's a tricky balance. Next-gen leaders don't want our teams to feel like they can't be human at work, and unless we're assholes, we want to create inclusive and equitable environments. We also want to manage folks' expectations. In spite of everything they want it to be, work simply cannot be the only place they find meaning. In service of that, we want to create literal and metaphorical space for them to find meaning outside of work.

A job is not meant to solve *all* your problems. Just as the workplace is not the right place for every version of you as a leader, the workplace is not the right institution or structure to deal with every part of someone's life.

We're going to start by defining what the role of work is and why it matters to be crystal clear about what you can and cannot deliver for folks. Then we'll get into a series of policies and norms you can consider setting, including how to think about hybrid/remote work environments, inclusivity, and bringing politics to work—all with a lens of inclusivity.

* * *

Over the last decade, many workplaces have changed to become more than just a place where you do the work then leave.

Part of that is by design: Some companies have shifted to provide even more "benefits" that ostensibly serve the employees but really aim to serve the company. Think the free meals or laundry services major tech companies provide or workout classes at the office that actually keep you chained to your desk.

Other companies have created programs like wellness support, personal-development opportunities, and baked-in socializing, all in response to staff feedback or stated desires. Don't get me wrong, some of these are good, helpful, and even delightful.

But many organizations have overpromised and understandably underdelivered because workplaces should not and cannot be responsible for meeting every possible need employees might have.

In his 2022 article "Building Resilient Organizations," Xennial Maurice Mitchell, national director of the Working Families Party, broke down some of the major problems facing progressive organizations and institutions at the time, including what he called "unanchored care."

Maurice defines this as:

> Assuming one's mental, physical, and spiritual health is the responsibility of the organization or collective space. The onus is on the organization to deal with the harm, burnout, or psychological stress one may experience through the work.

His assessment of the fallacies of unanchored care are precise:

> Discerning what is yours to hold and what is the collective's is an essential life skill and fundamental to organizational

> work, collaboration, and meaningful engagement of others. Organizations generally do not have the specialized skills to provide emotional or spiritual healing. Workplaces can provide a salary, benefits, paid time off, and other resources to help individuals access the support and care they require. Workplaces can also promote a culture of care and encourage individuals to care for themselves. Workplaces and colleagues cannot replace medical professionals, spiritual supports, or other devoted spaces of care. . . .
>
> Emotional intelligence is a capacity an organization can and should embody. But no organization can take on the emotional labor that is squarely in the domain of the individual. This distinction is critical.

While he was speaking purely about the progressive politics, nonprofit, and organizing spaces he operates in, I heard this problem come up in conversations with folks in medicine, education, corporate work, retail, legal services, and elsewhere. There is almost no sector that seems to be untouched by this challenge.

The solution is straightforward: As a leader, you need to have a clear and realistic understanding of what your company does and does not have a responsibility to do for your team, and in turn, you need to make that understanding clear to them.

Now I've got a take here: First and foremost, work is for money. By definition, a job is an economic relationship between employer and employee—one person's productivity in exchange for financial compensation (and, in the United States, usually health care).

There's a scene from *Mad Men* I find myself referencing a lot when I think about this.

In season 4, episode 7, "The Suitcase" (which is arguably one of the best episodes of the show), Don and Peggy are up late at the office working on a pitch for a suitcase company, and Peggy has missed a birthday dinner with her boyfriend and family to work on the assignment. She's understandably mad about it, on top of previous resentment against Don for not giving her credit for work on a previous project.

They go back and forth for a bit, as Peggy recounts the process of her brainstorming ideas, one of which Don then turned into an ultimately award-winning commercial.

The argument hits a climax:

Don: It's your job! I give you money, you give me ideas!

Peggy: And you never say thank you.

Don [yelling]: That's what the money's for!

Of course, work is not *just* about money—work provides meaning, can be a source of dignity, and creates structure for our lives. Anyone who's ever been unemployed, underemployed, or unhappily employed for a period of time can attest that the great empty nothingness of a day can feel not just daunting but horrifying. Unemployment actively causes emotional distress.[3]

But Don is speaking to a greater point: Sometimes, even under the absolute best of conditions (which you, as a leader, should aim to create), work sucks. That's why it's called work. And that, both literally and metaphorically, is what the money's for.

You can't solve every problem, and throwing money at employees will *never* excuse a hostile or discriminatory work environment, but ideally, you can pay people well enough and create enough of a structure around them so they have the resources—financially and in the form of time and flexibility—to solve their own problems.

Your goal as leader is not to provide for every possible want or need. Your goal is to create psychological and emotional safety, within reason, in order to serve the organization's goals and give people their dignity. That safety comes not from the mission or the work itself, but from the culture you create and the ways you assure expectations and reality are aligned.

You *do* have the responsibility to pay people well, in line with both market rates and what is needed to live and work within the geographic area you and they are located in. You have a responsibility to provide the best benefits you can afford given the realities of your business and in line with your organization's values. You have a responsibility to set clear guardrails and boundaries, so people can work to live, not necessarily live to work, and you have the obligation to treat people like people, not cogs in a machine.

You do not have the responsibility to make every day at work a trip to Disneyland. You do not have the responsibility to fulfill every person's full social, emotional, and physical needs every single day. You do not have the responsibility nor likely the skills to solve their mental or physical health problems, and you probably do not have the capacity to be their primary entry point for civic engagement. It's not your job to create the parameters of their social life.

It is also worth asking yourself: Which services are you providing that *should* be the responsibility of the government, and by providing them yourself, are you giving the government an out not to do so? For example, childcare. In an ideal world, companies that are not *literally childcare providers* would not provide childcare, because one of the many things we've learned from the health-care system as currently set up is that tying a necessary service to employment can create frustrating power dynamics—at best—and outright dangerous ones—at worst. We should aim to pay people well enough so they can comfortably afford childcare, and advocate as a company or as an individual (or both) for childcare to be exponentially more affordable, universally accessible, and funded by the government. (Now that being said, in the real world we live in, where it seems less and less likely that the government will ever pass policies to make childcare more affordable, providing it is ultimately good for the company's bottom line. So go forth and provide the benefits if you can swing it, and try not to be an asshole about it.)[4]

It can feel shitty to say, "This is not our problem to fix—it's yours." But pretending otherwise sets everyone up to fail.

* * *

All that being said: There are absolutely problems you *can* solve. One of my favorite people to talk to on this topic is millennial Danielle Curtis, the senior manager of employee experience and hybrid workplace at DonorsChoose.

DonorsChoose is an incredible organization that picks up the slack in our broken public-education system by creating easy ways for teachers to create wish lists of supplies that donors and philanthropists can then buy for them, instead of our government fully funding our public-education system like it should.

DonorsChoose has more than two hundred employees and a hybrid work environment. Danielle's full-time job is to think about the employee experience through that context. She's put more effort and intentionality into this than probably anyone you know.

Danielle described the complications of setting boundaries when telling me a story of how she had folks on her team asking for some kind of wellness program. They suggested a specific steps challenge, like with Fitbits or Apple Watch movement goals. She pushed back, explaining:

"When it comes to wellness, I'm not thinking about whether we should encourage a specific kind of physical wellness. I'm thinking about, does your job make you miserable? Do you need more support to be able to tackle some of the tougher parts of your work? Do you have enough time for recovery? Do you feel like your work is manageable? I'm thinking about stress—I'm not thinking about a steps challenge."

Often leaders can get stuck when responding to staff feedback or requests, thinking that the specific thing they want is the only acceptable answer. I'm not saying you should ignore your team, but your responsibility is to take a step back and ask: What is it they are really trying to solve for?

Danielle also considered a reframing of the broader question: We shouldn't be asking employees for their reactions to "Can I bring my full self to work?" Rather, we should be asking them to respond to: "Do I feel comfortable here?" The ideal answer is "Yes, and I'm challenged in a way I find exciting!"

Her biggest takeaway (and mine) around how to actually set expectations, articulate internal norms, and define which responsibilities fall on the company versus the individual is a simple one: "Make the implicit explicit."

Danielle explained that, based on her experience, people need permission more than you would think. They want to know what is acceptable and what isn't—you might assume that simply saying something like "Take lunch" is enough and that the boss doing so might show people you mean it, but in reality, you have to define what that means and how it looks and give people a system to rely on.

Another way to think about it, inspired by Priya Parker's must-read *The Art of Gathering*: Much like hosting a party and needing to articulate the dress code, you have to define what "acceptable" is—otherwise, at this metaphorical party, some people might come in shorts and others might show up in tuxedos, and no one will feel comfortable.

That might mean literally creating language to give people a framework. For example, Danielle and her team noticed that while the DonorsChoose policy was to encourage and empower people to take time out of their day to deal with personal business as needed (for example: pick their kids up from school at 2:00 p.m. because the school calendar has not yet adapted to the realities of working parents . . .), people were still hesitant to do it because they felt some kind of stigma or shame about blocking out their calendars.

So they came up with a phrase for it: golden time. If you needed to do something of a personal nature, you could just block out "golden time" on your calendar. This made it seem both admirable and acceptable because there was destigmatizing language for it.

• • •

Ask yourself: Which cultural norms are implied for your team that you can make explicit?

A few examples:

- If, like at DonorsChoose, your hope is that people use their calendars to block out personal time and manage others' expectations of availability, do you have specific language you can give folks to use to ensure cross-team consistency?

- If your communications norms are that people answer emails promptly—have you defined what "prompt" means?

- If your dress code is simply "business casual" or "look professional," how can you more explicitly define that?

- You've told people, "Don't be an asshole," as part of your code of conduct. What does "asshole" mean?

Write it all down. Literally. All of it, every word. This can feel silly with a small team or in an informal work environment; I chafed against it at first because it can start to feel like what I call "process-process bullshit" or like you're infantilizing grown-ups who should know what "prompt" means.

But it's absolutely necessary, especially if your team grows or if you find yourself dealing with underperformance or conflict. Having rules and policies to point to lets you lean on an agreement that someone has not abided by.

The alternative is like playing a card game for the first time but not learning a critical rule until the game was already over and you had lost. Without clarity up front, everyone is set up to fail.

I think about this the same way I think about the tactic of using the 6:00 p.m. church bells as a signal to my kid that it's time to leave the playground: "The bells toll for thee, kid! Time to go." The policies are what they are; the bells ring when they ring—we've all agreed to follow those signals, and now we have to stick with that.

Now, big red siren emoji here: This is an opportunity for inequity to rear its ugly, omnipresent head. Every step of codification of team culture introduces a chance for a dominant culture (usually white supremacy, the patriarchy, or both) to define the norms of a space that leaves some people feeling further disconnected. Creating processes for feedback and giving people explicit and implicit permission to call out your fuckups will help mitigate some of this.

Maurice Mitchell described this work to me as "building systems that anticipate that people are going to have bad days—that people are going to harm each other, that people are going to mistreat each other, that people are going to make mistakes"—and noted that "people" includes leaders. You want your processes to be compassionate and humane, but don't mistake that for weak or flimsy. Consider the house metaphor from earlier: You want your foundation (aka your systems) to be strong enough to withstand any kind of earthquake or bulldozer.

* * *

The need to be explicit about what the organization is and is not is hard enough in any workplace. In a remote workspace, it's both exponentially more difficult and more important. And it's absolutely necessary to figure it out because, based on employee demands and current research, it's highly likely you're going to have to lead a full or partial virtual team.

The return-to-office (RTO) mandate hit hard in early 2025 with a number of major corporations (and the federal government) requiring employees to work in person. That only further clarified the debate: By late 2025, 88 percent of employers still provided some hybrid work options and 67 percent of companies offer some level of flexibility.[5] The workforce is even more eager for some kind of flexibility.[6] (And consider: Something like the PTA, where much of the work happens outside of in-person meetings, is comparable to a remote work environment.) This is all complicated by Gen Z, who have the most complex relationship with remote work by far, with only 23 percent preferring fully remote workplaces. I suspect this is true in part because many of the fully remote companies have not built in enough structures for Gen Z employees to feel part of something or connect with their colleagues. Still, as you manage people, you will benefit by erring on the side of flexibility and setting things up so everyone can thrive.

For simplicity's sake, I'm going to use "remote" as a term to encompass all the varieties of the state of the office: workplaces that are entirely online, workplaces that have an office but include a few days of working from home, and workplaces that are primarily in person but have a few members of the team working remotely—any combination that isn't 100 percent in person 100 percent of the time.

I'm admittedly a remote-work enthusiast, having done so since early 2017. I love it all: no commuting, more flexibility in my schedule, the time to quickly sweep up the seemingly unending amounts of dog kibble on the floor in between meetings, and my personal favorite perk, the freedom to squeeze in a Peloton ride in the tiny window of time between when my husband takes the kids to day care and my first meeting of the day.

I can be physically comfortable in my environment. I get to spend as much time as possible with my family. I eat home-cooked meals more. Since I spend so much of my day on the phone, anyway, I can often take my calls while sitting on our balcony or out walking the dog.

But having said all that, I know (and studies prove) remote work is not for everyone nor every type of work, and it can be challenging for folks at both ends of the org chart. For junior staff or people entering the workforce for the first time, it can be isolating, hard to learn team culture, harder to find mentors or build relationships, and harder still to prove merit.

For leaders, management in a remote environment requires more of everything: more time, more intentionality, more communication, more clarity, more feedback loops. Next-gen leaders, per usual, have it harder because we don't have a ton of examples on how to do this well: The aforementioned and all-too-common boomer style of "management by walking around" has always been ridiculous, and it's particularly laughable in the modern work environment.

* * *

The remote office is analogous to TikTok or any other algorithmically defined social media platform—each person's experience of it is structurally the same, meaning we're all swiping up or down, but simultaneously, we're having fundamentally different exposure (e.g., I'm hate-watching clips of snake eggs hatching while you're watching people do home renovations).

In an in-person office, everyone enters the same physical space, shaped by the same norms—people leave for lunch, or use headphones, or show off pictures of their pets in their cubicles, or whatever. The office decor gives a sense of how the organization defines itself—cool, or formal, or bro-ey, etc. The forced proverbial watercooler interactions with people you might not otherwise collaborate with have some work benefit and some social benefit and help dictate what the vibes of the office are.

In a remote team, there is no lobby to shape how you feel when you walk into the office. There is no shared space beyond a Slack team or comparable chat system—few people have the same experience of a day; there is no common "someone microwaved fish in the kitchen" story to bond over. My experience of my workplace is wildly different from that of any person on my team, even and including my equal cofounder, based fully on whom we interact with and the one-to-one or one-to-few communications we're on.

So as the leaders, we have to be explicit about what shared experiences or behaviors can rise to the top of everyone's metaphorical office FYP—what does the "office algorithm" embrace, and what does it reject?

The overarching action item is simple: Say the thing. You probably already have organization values or a team charter—if not, rectify that and get writing. Put pen to paper on how you want people to perform, how you want them to treat one another, and what it means to be on the team.

If you're not sure where to start, look at what's already happening. Danielle at DonorsChoose told me how when they were going through the process of reevaluating the organization's values, she noticed that their Slack team had hundreds of iterations of custom emojis for "thank you." Gratitude seemed to be baked into the DonorsChoose values—so they made it explicit as part of the organization's stated operating ethos.

Consider what all-staff spaces you've got: Whether it's all-team Slack channels, email LISTSERVs, or regular all-hands meetings, those are intentional places to both model and explicitly name (and rename) organization culture.

One thing Run for Something has done that I love and am so proud of: We have a strong culture of celebration. That comes up in an all-staff Slack channel literally called #celebrations, where we highlight both people's personal moments of glory (birthdays! work anniversaries!) and professional accomplishments (an amazing training someone held or a compliment from an outside partner that made its way to us!).

We also end every all-staff meeting with a ritual of celebrating colleagues. We call it our Fionas (after Fiona the hippo at the Cincinnati Zoo; there's a whole spiel about her that my cofounder will recount anytime new staff start). Each meeting, three people who were the Fionas in the previous meeting name other folks on staff who have done something excellent. It's comparable to an employee-of-the-month celebration but driven from the bottom up (or middle out) instead of from the top down.

I'm aggressively intentional about participating in those spaces. Similarly, I like to celebrate people who take vacation or use our sabbatical policy. Even if I'm not always great about it myself (more on that later), the things we celebrate and lift up in the metaphorical office algorithm are the things that others replicate.

• • •

Part of the massive shift to remote work over the last decade was due to the pandemic. Arguably, however, the pandemic simply expedited something that was already in the works due to technology. A decade ago, there wasn't the same proliferation of cheap and widely available tools that would allow for multiuser chatting, video calls, screen shares, and other nuts and bolts that are now essential to the modern (white-collar) workplace.

That's amazing. It also opens up new avenues of possible chaos in a team.

As Slack (a term I'm using to mean all kinds of online chat systems) becomes the shared office space, who gets to define the boundaries of a group at work have changed. Anyone can create a private chat without leadership knowing in a way that would have been noticed in an office environment, where a dozen folks gathering in a conference room would have raised a few questions.

Generally speaking, this is great. Companies that have seen "reckonings," usually for the better, have seen them foment via private Slack channels, DMs, and group chats. It's valuable for people (especially those seeking to rectify inequities in the workplace) to have ways to communicate.

However, keep in mind that people may be a little more audacious in Slack chats or in a Zoom chat than they might be face-to-face. Consider how you use video chats and phone calls as ways to foster intimacy between teammates of various levels. It's unfortunately very easy to be shitty to someone—intentionally or not—via text chat in a way that's much harder when you can see their expressions.

There is a balance to strike between building relationships and creating equitable and accessible environments, and there is no one right answer. I have generally found that in moments of tension, seeing people's faces helps lower the temperature a bit.

When you do have people turning into virulent keyboard warriors, it's incumbent on you as leadership to nip it in the bud immediately and, if necessary, in a public way. As workplaces become essentially online communities, you (or, more practically, someone you delegate this responsibility to) have to function as a community moderator, in the same way a Facebook group or Reddit moderator might.

The key steps here include:

Having a clear code of conduct. Again, make the implicit explicit. Especially with younger members of your team, you may need to overtly teach them how to act. Emily Reilly, a millennial high school principal turned school system administrator, explained that she literally ran "interaction trainings" with her staff on how to use technology to communicate with parents. "You got this text message. How do you respond?" she'd ask her trainees, explaining to me that "a lot of them respond very angrily in the moment, and that is obviously not professional or appropriate."

Have a clear escalation path. If someone says something out of line or against your code of conduct, how do you hold them accountable? While I generally err on the side of praise publicly and critique privately, when it comes to enforcing communication norms, once you've established what "good" and "bad" are, you can't hesitate.

Start with one or two private warnings, then move it to a public space if needed. You want to strike a balance between assuming good intentions and calling out bad behavior. Being unable to align with the organization's code of conduct can be a performance issue (or symptomatic of one), and you need to treat it with as much seriousness as you would a mistake on a data analysis or any other work product.

Model good behavior yourself—both in what you do proactively and what you do when you make a mistake. When you fuck up (as you inevitably will; we are all human) and violate the code of conduct, call yourself out and apologize. Show vulnerability. Give an example of how you'd like others to own up to their behavior, and create a permission structure for your team to do the same.

• • •

A remote team should still try to come together for in-person gatherings as much as financially or logistically possible. But outside of those, treat every time you're together as a chance to reinforce your norms.

That includes meetings. Whether it's video meetings or in-person sessions or retreats, don't waste the time you have when you're gathered as a group.

I know that for some people, meetings are the devil's work. Millennial Danielle Kantor, founder of consulting group Sticky Note Labs and an expert meeting facilitator herself, is the first to admit that meetings have become a shortcut around having other important structures in place: "We're all in way too many meetings and most of them without a clear purpose. Meetings aren't the problem—it's how we're using them."

A few hot tips:

Every meeting or retreat has to have a goal. It doesn't necessarily need to be a productive one; it can be as simple as "get to know one another," but make sure you have one and everyone attending the space knows it. Danielle explains, "If *you* don't know the goal and can't write an agenda, maybe your meeting *should* be an email."

It will feel counterintuitive, but you have to plan for spontaneity and synchronicity. Structure and agendas go a long way, as does intentional facilitation. That doesn't mean every minute is accounted for, but rather: When you know what the goal of a meeting is, you can quickly identify when moments that feel like they're going off the rails are actually just different ways of getting to the same destination.

Your participation as the boss needs to be carefully calibrated. A good example comes from Evan Spiegel, the millennial CEO and cofounder of Snap Inc. you met earlier, who worked with his team to create Council, a structured way of building empathy and relationships— people get together in small groups of at most fifteen people and take turns sharing about what's going on in their lives or responding to a prompt.

In a facilitated space, he explained, "The vast majority of time you spend in that circle, you're listening." He calls it an "incredibly effective way to build relationships," describing that teams that have done Council relate to one another totally differently from those that haven't. Even as the top top boss, he joins and is honest; he views it as an opportunity to both "speak from the heart and listen from the heart." It'd be easy for him to decide those spaces are for everyone else, not for him—instead, he leans all the way in and shows up 100 percent.

Use icebreakers. I'm personally a big fan of these. At Run for Something, we start every all-staff meeting with an icebreaker. Sometimes silly ones, sometimes thoughtful ones, sometimes a little bit in between. When the team was small, every member of the staff would answer the question in front of everyone else; now that we're bigger we break out into smaller groups and answer them among four to five people. We've also started sending around icebreakers with the agenda a few days before the meeting and now offer up two options of varying tones or intimacy to give people a choice of which they want to engage with.

Icebreakers can feel silly, and as the organization has grown and our all-staff meetings have gotten more jam-packed, there have been suggestions to do away with the ritual.

But experts generally agree that the chitchat before getting to work makes a difference. Consider what happens in an in-person office: You'd enter the conference room a few minutes before the meeting starts, grab a donut or piece of fruit off the tray or spruce up your coffee, and chat with someone about the weather, the local sports team, your kids, whatever. Small talk sucks in many ways, but it also allows for an entry point to deeper human connection. It gives you a way to get to know your teams as people first, employees second.

Danielle from Sticky Note Labs makes the case that icebreakers help equalize everyone in the space: "You don't know if a coworker on Zoom is coming out of a challenging meeting, is juggling child or elder care at home, or has been heads down on a project," she explained. "It starts you off at the same place, regardless of title."

She also notes that for meetings that are centered on collaboration and engagement (which, ideally, are most of them!), her goal is for everyone to "literally use their voice" within the first five to ten minutes. "Especially on Zoom: You have to go off mute, maybe go on camera, and engage in the conversation." That's the hard part—check, done. Icebreakers help break the seal (or, ahem, the ice) on participating in the conversation.

Icebreakers solve for the "small talk over Zoom sucks" problem. There's no simple way to wrap it up without feeling like an asshole, "ready to get down to business," and the cadences of normal conversation feel off. Get-to-know-you games function as structured small talk that you can both timebox and prepare for. It's an easy win.

Meetings are "culture-carriers" for organizations, as Danielle puts it—you can demonstrate how you respect and value people's time (and model good behavior) in group spaces. Don't waste your chance.

Everything we just went through—setting and calibrating the metaphorical remote workplace algorithm, codes of conduct and community moderation, using meetings as culture drivers—needs to be written down, codified, and repeated over and over again. In a remote work environment, you have to be vigilant about documentation and hammering it home for your team. In the same way your social media presence in an earlier chapter had to fit the narrative of "you, the person," your organization's communication norms and policies need to fit the narrative of "the organization, a place where people show up to get shit done."

• • •

Part of creating space for people to be their real selves (but not their full selves, unless they want to be) is being expansive about what *kinds* of people get to be their real selves. Spoiler: The answer should be nearly everyone.

One of the particular strengths and opportunities for next-gen leaders is a desire for inclusivity. Part of that is because so many of us don't look like or live like the leaders who came before us, we've been in spaces not meant for people like us, and we know how much feeling like we're not welcome sucks. Part of it is practicality: teams will get more diverse because the country is getting more diverse with each subsequent generation, and as leaders, we want our teams to succeed, so we want everyone to be able to do their best work.

I want to dispel with some bullshit here: While the federal government eliminated diversity, equity, and inclusion programs, and people proudly bragged about being able to use slurs in the workplace again (and in especially cowardly moves, dozens of Fortune 100 companies scaled back DEI language in their public filings), there is no ambiguity in the results. Diverse teams, *when run well*, make us all better. There are more opportunities for learning, more innovation, less of a chance of groupthink, and ultimately, better performance. I understand this might be a hot take in contemporary circles, but segregation is bad and inclusivity is good, actually. The political and legal landscape may make it harder to create equitable workplaces but those same conditions also make it more important.

The challenge is in that caveat: To reap the benefits, you have to run a diverse team well. The positive outcomes of heterogeneous teams come from *generative* conflict, and generative conflict can only come to fruition when there are extremely clear rules of engagement.

In *The Art of Gathering*, Priya Parker explains that diverse spaces require concrete codes of conduct. When spaces are homogenous, everyone is operating off the same assumptions and general cultural norms, so you can rely on implicit etiquette. When you're bringing people together from different backgrounds, you need explicit rules.

Perhaps counterintuitively, in order to be inclusive, you need to be just a little bit exclusive. You've got to set hard limits: I suggest no racists, no sexists, no bigots, no assholes. You won't always get this right, but you have to actively try. You've got to draw the lines in the sand and not tolerate it when people cross them.

This was best illustrated by my conversation with millennial Alli King, who teaches in North Carolina during the school year. In the summer, she runs an overnight camp for boys in the mountains. She's extremely open with parents, students, and campers about her own neurodivergence as someone diagnosed with ADHD, in no small part because it allows her to have very pointed conversations she otherwise wouldn't be able to engage in.

"I had kids [I was teaching] whose parents were less supportive of them as humans because of their diagnoses," Alli said sadly. Her neurodivergence allows her to be a better teacher to her kids and also be firmer about boundaries: "You can always tell when kids haven't had an ADHD teacher before because they'll be like, 'My ADHD means this and that,' with some kind of absurd thing," Alli explained. "You are still able to do your work. I don't care if you're sprawled on the floor under your desk doing your work, but you will do it." It's a tough love environment.

Similarly, when she and her team are presenting to parents about enrollment, she proactively brings up her own diagnosis because "I want parents to hear someone who's successful having it, that it's fine." That, in turn, draws a particular kind of camper and employee: Alli thinks their percentage of enrolled kids and staff with ADHD or autism may be higher than usual.

"We made a very specific business plan and did a lot of mission work before opening, so we have our values," Alli explained, pointing to some of the meaningful but "flowery" language they've got laid out. But it really shows up in behavior. "If you're not going to be okay with your kid painting their fingernails, then they don't need to come to our camp," she said, telling me a story of how a parent got mad that their son came home with painted nails and said they weren't going to send their kid back the next summer. "Okay, if that's the hill you're going to die on, then you're not for us," she recounted telling the parent.

"We have to be consistent about our values. When one camper was making fun of another for signing up for [fingernail painting]," Alli said, "we shut that down immediately." There is no tolerance in her camp for mocking someone else's creativity or self-expression.

She and her team were rigorous around creating an inclusive environment—that meant occasionally being exclusive. Much like with responsible authenticity, you have to know where you stand and what you believe.

Full honesty here: Diversity, equity, and inclusion work is a rigorous practice, and I am far from being an expert—but I have read a ton, learned a ton, and worked with some of the best practitioners in the field. To ensure I got this right, this particular section was informed and reviewed by Run for Something's chief diversity officer, Ciara Walton, who is one of the smartest thinkers I know about how to operationalize DEI initiatives and balance all the tensions at hand.

With her leadership and our intentionality, as we've scaled, Run for Something has worked hard to ensure our team reflects the candidates we work with, a specific goal we set in order to make us better at our mission. Within the first four years, our team was more than half people of color, including a leadership team that is a majority people of color and has stayed that way ever since.

We've established policies prioritizing equity and inclusion—for example, we have market-based, fully transparent salary bands with a no-negotiation policy for new hires (since research shows women and candidates of color tend to negotiate less than white men and then get paid less as a result), and we've set benchmarks for our hiring pools to ensure that we're always considering a diverse range of talent for any particular role.

We've built an in-house team of experts who advise, coach, and consult on internal and external work, assessing everything from data collection to language and style guides. We are constantly evaluating ourselves against our values and equity-centered practices. We haven't always gotten it all right, but we've absolutely tried.

I have two major takeaways from my personal experience:

Number one: Know what you don't know. Consider whose voices are being heard and whose voices are being overlooked, whether consciously or unconsciously. Which perspectives are you lacking? How can you fill those gaps?

Then, put your money where your values are. Hire experts or push for their hiring as full-time, long-term team members in senior positions equipped with the resources at their disposal to drive real change. Or, at the very least, bring experts on as outside consultants and fully empower them to make an impact.

Number two: Representation is a tactic in service of building equitable and inclusive spaces—it is not an end goal in and of itself.

Hiring and empowering people from different backgrounds—different races, classes, gender identities and sexual orientations, abilities, generations, and all the other ways you can name—is a necessary step toward equity. It's also not the only step. Especially for "nontraditional" (again, a term I'm using to mean usually non–white cisgender straight men) leaders, being elevated into power without support or structure can feel like being set up to fail.

This makes sense: These "nontraditional" leaders are entering spaces not created for people like them and are actively redefining ideas of power as they grapple with it themselves.

Stephanie Llanes, the millennial working as managing director at a major democracy-related nonprofit, remembers being told when she was first entering the workforce "how you're supposed to dress, how you're supposed to wear your hair, don't wear hoop earrings, don't wear your history"—over time, she's rejected those instructions and developed her own sense of authenticity in the workplace, but it hasn't been easy.

"There's things that, culturally, I'm not going to bring to work," she said, describing the Puerto Rican tradition of greeting people with hugs and kisses on the cheek. But she is unapologetic about who she is—a mom, a Latina, a lawyer, an executive, who can be incredibly good at her job and also wear excellent earrings on the Zoom call.

Stephanie is modeling showing up as her real self and creating space for other leaders and members of the team to do the same.

And yet, as Samhita Mukhopadhyay put it in her book *The Myth of Making It*, putting people in leadership positions without supporting them in actually changing the systems runs the risk of reproducing the same inequalities. These leaders must have the power and resources to drive real change.

Alida Garcia, from our conversation on social media, is also one of the left's leaders on diversifying the talent pipeline. Her perspective on representation is nuanced: "Organizations have missions, and the diversity to meet the mission of one organization might be different than that of the next."

She also addressed something I've felt personally as a white woman in a position of power: "With white leaders, they feel like, 'Well, I'm a white boss. So barring me leaving, what does inclusion and equity look like?' The answer isn't always that they need to leave," Alida explained. Rather, we need to recognize our unconscious biases, understand the systemic inequalities deeply ingrained in our society, and acknowledge our privileges. Then we have to do the work as leaders to make sure our systems are equitable, that we have clear frameworks for professional development and delegation, look at pay and benefits, and more. She went on: "There are infinite ways to look at this work, and I think that's where people get overwhelmed. . . . People can feel like they're spinning in circles and there's no end to it. [But] that's the point."

All that being said, here are a few more things you can do or consider as you work to ensure you're creating a workplace that is equitable, diverse, and inclusive:

Do the reading (and keep doing it). As the leader, you have a responsibility to educate yourself on the current best practices around equity and inclusion. This is a rigorous field of knowledge, practices, and tactics that you can proactively learn, in the same way that budgeting, copy writing, or coding are things you can learn. No matter how much you think you know, you can always know more. Don't assume that just because you've experienced racism or sexism, or you've been underpaid, or you've dealt with microaggressions that you know how to structurally and culturally prevent it in your own workplace. Your lived experience might shape your prioritization of this work, but it doesn't automatically make you an expert in it.

It's also important to recognize the necessity of unlearning—challenging and letting go of outdated beliefs or biases you might hold. Things we were previously raised to believe or misconceptions and beliefs that we've held over time should be questioned, challenged, and let go.

Bake inclusivity into your team values and norms in every functional area. This is not just about hiring practices or compensation (although it absolutely needs to be considered in those components of your work!). Consider how you evaluate things like your communication norms, technology, and accessibility, the events you host, the literal work you do—everything. There are small ways you can make a big difference in inclusivity: One person I spoke with explained how when she was invited to speak on a panel at a conference, the host included in the email invitation details like exactly what kind of accessibility the stage had, what type of chairs she'd be sitting on, and other accommodations—all without knowing what the invitee might need. There is no downside to that kind of gesture, and it made the invitee know she was entering a space that was thoughtful about who could participate.

If it matters, measure it and then evaluate it. If you want to get better, you need to know where you're starting from—and putting numbers to it all can make a huge difference. For example, if your goal is to increase diversity within your team, you need to first assess your current demographics to identify gaps. If you want to improve team morale and inclusivity, conducting a survey can provide a baseline for how your team currently feels about the workplace. There are countless examples here of things you can measure, and the ways in which you measure them should be informed by an expert in this field. Don't be afraid to confront the data, even if it reveals significant challenges—this is an opportunity to recognize how much potential there is for positive change.

Have grace and also have no tolerance. These two principles might seem contradictory, but they are two sides of the same coin. Conversations about race, gender, power dynamics, and identity are constantly evolving—ideas that are normal today may have been radical or theoretical just a few years ago. There are huge gaps in understanding around these topics that can leave some folks—particularly those from an older generation or from different educational backgrounds—feeling like they're constantly getting it wrong or falling behind. People are going to make mistakes. You're going to make mistakes! Give some grace for those errors and recognize that this is a learning process.

However, extending grace doesn't mean allowing racism, sexism, bigotry, or hostility to go unchecked. While intentions are important, the impact of someone's actions is even more crucial. One clear way to show team members you're serious about creating inclusive environments is showing no tolerance when someone egregiously or blatantly crosses the line.

Finally, don't give up. Working to create an inclusive team environment can feel like an effort doomed to fail: You will never get it perfectly right, someone will always be offended or feel silenced, and there are always more land mines to step on. There are leaders who don't even try for equity (or even the opposite: They try to proactively be racist, sexist, bigoted, or otherwise dickish), and because they put in no effort, no one expects better of them. It can be tempting to look at the unending to-do list and opt out entirely—it can feel similar to arguing with my toddler, where the only way to win the game is not to play. Do not give up. In an era where diversity and equity work is being punished—a not-so-subtle effort at kicking women and people of color out of the workforce—be brave. I know everyone will have a different risk tolerance and your calculations may not be as clear cut as mine, but I hope you will hear me when I say: History will not look fondly on leaders who fold on this.

Try anyway. Intentionally building a diverse team—whatever diverse means for your circumstances—and creating space for productive conflict will ensure you can all be more creative, make better decisions, and have fewer blind spots. All of this is in service of your goal, so it's worth the effort.

• • •

This is going to seem to be in direct tension with the guidelines for creating inclusive and welcoming workspaces, but it's true, so let's talk about it: You need to create space for politics at work.

It's simply unavoidable. The political environment has become so all-encompassing and intersects with so many other topics—sports, health care, housing, religion, books, music, fashion—that there is no way to draw a clear distinction between political topics and everything else.

I know this is uncomfortable—bringing politics to work has gotten Messy with a capital *M*.

Multiple things are happening at the same time:

1. Gen Z is entering the workforce wanting to work at places that reflect their political affiliations or values, whether appropriate or not for the industry. Similarly, Gen Zers (and millennials) want to spend their money on brands that align with their values.

2. Politics is getting more fucked up (to say the least), and nonpolitical organizations and companies feel an obligation to weigh in, both morally and/or for profit; see point one.

3. The demise of civic institutions pushes people to want more political community out of their employer because they can't find it elsewhere.

And yet: Work cannot be someone's political or civic home. This is true in corporate America and possibly even more true in a mission-driven industry. Hell, I work in politics, and my political job is not always my political home. Not everything I want to do fits within the mission of the organization I literally built from the ground up; that doesn't mean what I believe (or what the organization does) is definitionally wrong.

Rather, it's that there are political actions I may want to take or show support for (for example, foreign policy issues that have no clear connection to our work in local politics or advocacy on behalf of a gubernatorial candidate that has no ties to the organization) that I need to find time for outside of my day job.

Even in the most values-aligned role, your work (or your volunteer effort) is simply not the place to satisfy everything you want to do to make the world better. Consider Louise Yeung, millennial chief climate officer in the New York City comptroller's office.

Her job involves using the levers available to her—budget analysis, policy research, contract approvals, financial controls, accountability measures, and the like—to further the city's efforts to fight against and prepare for climate change. While the work is incredibly urgent, like any government or bureaucratic role change can be very slow. Louise has to sit with that tension, reminding herself that, as activist Mariame Kaba puts it, "hope is a discipline," and in the same vein, anger can be a fuel for action.

But as she put it, her work is "not necessarily the only container" for all she wants to accomplish. She has a creative practice—a mix of visual art, printmaking, painting, and public-space activations—that allows her to push a cultural conversation around climate change beyond what she can do from her purview in city government.

It's not that her work isn't meaningful or valuable. Rather, it simply isn't everything. "My creative practice and my professional practice are equally important to the way that I'd like to show up in the world," Louise explained. "My creative practice allows me to ask similar questions that I explore at work but answer them in very different ways." She's up-front about it with both her boss and her team: Louise has had to navigate conflict-of-interest waivers for some outside activities and sets aside time to go to the art studio or do artist residencies as appropriate.

She does all this for herself to maintain her balance, but also to model that not being able to solve *every* climate problem through the tools available to them in the city comptroller's office does not mean that they can't tackle other problems outside of it. The place you get your paycheck can't be the only place you're agitating for action.

The specifics of politics in the workplace—and how you as a leader handle it—will vary depending on where you are, what you do, and the issues at hand.

Just my two cents: If you have the latitude to push the limits on political speech and action within the confines of your mission and goals, you should. We are quite obviously no longer in the world of Aaron Sorkin, where democracy is a given and bipartisanship or neutrality is an objective good. Standing for something, even if it results in some backlash, can have brand benefits. I think a lot of a scene in Taylor Swift's *Miss Americana* documentary where she describes her anxiety around making a political endorsement and the hate she'd likely get. She couldn't live with staying quiet as a political leader said hateful things about so many of her friends and fans. She asked herself: What was her platform for if not to use it for good? If you have any modicum of influence or power that can strategically be put to good use, do it. I encourage a little bit of risk tolerance here, as much as is appropriate. Your cost-benefit analysis may be complicated as the powers that be use political disagreements as an excuse to cut off funding or legally punish leaders and companies. But I hope you'll be honest about your actual exposure and consider the benefits of speaking out as well as the possible drawbacks.

The thing to keep in mind is that your personal political values, while important, are less relevant than the organization's goals, which is why having extreme clarity on what you're hoping to accomplish is helpful to lean on when deciding which action to take or not take.

This came up in a conversation with Amanda Herring, a millennial working as executive director of the Jewish student organization, Hillel, at Virginia Tech. She started the job in August 2023, and then in October, the war in Israel and Palestine escalated. All of a sudden, she was balancing staff who had family in Israel, students who were dealing with the complicated emotions at play, protests and encampments on campus, pressure from news outlets and parents, and more.

She explained, "It's important to help [the staff] see when you code switch—when you're talking to the administration, when you're talking to parents, when you're talking to the media." She was very clear with her team: "This is our message as Hillel. You're allowed to have personal values, but you need to understand when what you say is representing *you* and when what you say is representing *the organization*."

This is a tough thing for new leaders to learn and can be even tougher for employees to understand. I've struggled with this over the years as employees have asked us to make statements on issues that simply do not overlap with Run for Something's work and, in some circumstances, might even compromise it—even if I personally agree with the stand our team is asking us to take, I have to say no.

If it does not positively serve our candidates, then it is not our place to do it, whatever it is, full stop. And as the public spokesperson of the organization, I have to be extra cautious: I've seen my random tweets pop up in the press as quotes. I have to tread carefully.

If you find that where you work and what you personally believe become incompatible, take the necessary steps to move on, which is easier said than done but also rarely impossible if given a long enough time horizon. This is similarly true for your team. If they want more politics out of their job than you as an employer can provide, then this is no longer the right job for them. If you can legally say that in the kindest way possible, you should.

As you are creating or redefining team culture, consider a few things as they relate to politics . . .

What space are you creating for people to have political or civic engagement outside of work? Do you give paid time off for voting? What about volunteering? Do you, as the leader, model taking time? Do you remind people about upcoming voter-registration deadlines and election days? I'd argue this is the bare minimum, but it's also more than a lot of places do, so do it if you can.

Give people permission to step away. Over the years as major news events have occurred—from police violence against Black people to foreign conflicts to mass shootings and, sadly, so much more—we've reiterated to our team: If what's going on in the world is making it hard for you to do your job, step away for a few hours or a day. You don't need to give an excuse; just let your manager know you need some time and block out your calendar. Acknowledging what's going on, naming that it's hard and that some people might be affected more than others and that they can log off at any time to care for themselves goes a long way. Occasionally we'll have people take us up on it, but most of the time, it's simply appreciated that we called it out in the first place.

What kind of guidelines can you create around political discussion? It's going to happen, so do what you can to lower the temperature. If you've done the work to create an inclusive environment, then you've got the structures to lean on—reinforce those codes of conduct.

Do your values align with your actions? If your organization, for example, lists "anti-racist" as one of your values, then speaking up against racism and injustice falls under that bucket. If one of your values is "pushing boundaries and disrupting the old way of doing things," then there are political actions one might expect from you. Google's infamous "Don't be evil" motto came into tension with a ton of work Google does (which I imagine is part of why they removed it from their code of conduct in 2018). When they were operating under that ethos, it was totally reasonable for employees at Google to be like, "Hey, seems like we're doing an evil thing. I thought we didn't do that here."

It is imperative to hold a boundary about what kind of political engagement is acceptable in the workplace and what kind of politics your team can expect from you (the leader) and you (the company). Once again: Clarity is the name of the game.

• • •

Creating a workplace where people can be their real selves but not necessarily their full selves starts with day one: onboarding.

There's a theme currently in vogue in millennial parenting (although I have to assume not exclusive to millennial parenting) about prepping your kids before experiences that may be new, scary, or alarming. Think: in the days leading up to a doctor's appointment, reading books about going to the doctor, talking through exactly what the day will look and feel like, and getting a fake stethoscope and real-but-fun Band-Aid to put on Elmo to show the kid what will happen at the appointment.

Or consider how you think about sending invitations to an event. Invites are not just logistics; they're a chance to set the tone and vibe for the day. A wedding invite that comes with beautiful satin-lined envelopes and delicate lace wrapped around the thick embossed card stock sets a very different mood than an e-vite, no matter how glamorous the e-vite. (I say this with no judgment: We did Gmail invites for our wedding!)

Translate this to your leadership role. How can you best prepare people for what they're going to experience?

It starts with the job description. Most people don't spend enough time on these, and most don't consider them as a tool to use even outside paid employment. If you're running a volunteer team for a local dog rescue, write a job description for every type of volunteer you need!

Your MO here is "make it easy for people to say yes!" and it's much easier for them to say yes if they know exactly what will and will not be required of them. Be specific and clear about what the responsibilities of the role will be and what success looks like in it. Even better, at least once a year, as part of re-onboarding, do a job description audit: Work with your team to evaluate their work against their job description and see if what you included is actually what they're doing and what's changed.

That change isn't necessarily bad, but you don't want it to happen without documenting it, and you'll be better able to identify which roles you need in the future if you're accurately capturing what each team member is actually doing. This is also a useful way to gut check prioritization, time management, and which balls might have gotten dropped as expectations meet reality.

You're not just teaching someone new what the work is; you're teaching them how the culture operates. Steph Cheng, the tech leader you met in part one, explained how the first three months of someone joining a team are when they're both the most malleable and most vulnerable—you can set the foundation for how you want them to show up.

Especially with team members who may be new to the workforce, Steph will shadow them in some meetings or collaborate more with them and talk through it all in a way that encourages self-awareness and self-reflection. "We'll do a little debrief after every meeting, and I'll be like: 'What felt good?'—and it's always on them first to say what went well and what could have been better. Then I'll give my assessment on their assessment." You've got a lot of leeway in the first few months to give feedback that may be harder to communicate later on without it getting contentious or misunderstood. Don't miss your opportunity.

Manage everyone's expectations to understand that good onboarding takes time. I love a good trial by fire as much as the next crazy person, but it's not fair to someone new to the team to expect them to be up to speed by the end of the first week, or even the end of the first month. There are formal tools you can leverage like a 30/60/90, in which you as the leader detail out what the new person should be learning and doing thirty days into the role, sixty days into the role, and then ninety days into the role. Using this may feel like process-process bullshit, but it can be very helpful for both you and the new person as you think intentionally about how that ramp-up will feel.

I like to tell new members of our team: In the first month, you're going to feel simultaneously overwhelmed with information and also bored, without much to do, and like you're not sure why you're here. In the second month, you'll start to get the hang of it. By the end of the third month, you'll be so busy you've forgotten what that boredom of month one felt like. That's a good sign.

Normalize a re-onboarding process. KP Trueblood, millennial president of the Brooklyn Museum in New York City, explained that she goes one step further and is regularly encouraging a re-onboarding process—she has current team members regularly go through the welcome-to-the-team experience themselves, reaffirming the organization's values and updating themselves on how things work. I love this idea and plan on bringing it to my organization; consider doing the same (and using it as an excuse to regularly update all your onboarding materials).

• • •

Stepping back for a quick recap—so far we've covered:

- Clear boundaries and expectations about what people can expect from their workplace.
- The need for explicit behavioral norms.
- How to set up a flexible work environment that allows people to be full people outside their jobs.
- The need for group spaces and meetings that drive forward team culture.

- What to consider as you design inclusive and equitable policies.
- The imperative to create metaphorical containers for politics at work.
- Why a well-run onboarding (and re-onboarding) process can make or break it all.

If you've got all those things in motion, you're well on your way to creating a workplace where your team can hit the jackpot of accomplishing their goals and being their real selves at work while not ever having to be their full selves.

You've set everyone (including yourself!) up to succeed by plainly laying out what work is and is not for. You've laid the foundation for a workplace that *can* be joyful, meaningful, intellectually stimulating, emotionally fulfilling, and a sustaining source of dignity but doesn't lose sight of the reality that work is an economic relationship first and foremost. (And if your leadership isn't at work, then congrats, you're running the best adult soccer league in the history of soccer leagues.)

That's huge. But it's only one half of the equation. You also have to consider how you're setting up time for people to live full lives outside of work. Keep reading.

IN ORDER TO WORK BETTER, YOU NEED TO REST BETTER

Raise your hand or roll your eyes if you've heard some variation of this before: "Kids these days just don't want to work anymore."

It feels like every few weeks, some article, video, or viral social media post comes out ranting about how millennials and Gen Zers are lazy, good-for-nothing brats. They're always trying to log off right when the clock hits 5:00 p.m. (even though they're not paid for work after 5:00 p.m.), they're serious about not answering emails over vacation (even though paid vacation days are part of the benefits package provided by the company), and they don't dare to work through the flu (even though rest is necessary for healing). Those piece-of-shit next-gen team members want to work for the hours they're paid for and then leave to go pick up their kids, fit in a workout, or lounge around in pajamas scrolling the internet for three hours before bed. Monsters, the ranters say, absolute monsters!!

Obviously I think those rants are ridiculous. Too many of us got our starts in workplaces where the idea of living a full life outside of work was frowned upon for junior members of the team and was often poorly modeled by leadership. Millennial and Gen Z workers are rejecting that work *has* to be that way—as next-gen leaders, we can take the next steps to turn that sentiment into structural support for rest.

Let's break that cycle. We have a responsibility to be intentional about what many people call work-life balance but I prefer to think of it as work-rest integration. After all, we work what feels like (or is!) a vast majority of our waking hours—what is work if not a major part of life?

We need to be thinking about creating space for work and rest, about giving people not just permission to unplug but active guardrails to guide them on how to do it.

Liz Zaretsky, a millennial running the online fundraising efforts at the New York Public Library, summed this up well, describing her leadership style as one that revolved around the idea that "the life of everyone I manage should not be miserable. First, work is great, but it's not all that matters, and so you simply should not be miserable at the thing you are doing with most of your waking hours. Second, I actually do think people are better at their jobs when they're not miserable."

She has explicit fundraising goals she needs her team to hit, and she holds them accountable for doing so. But those goals, she believes, should not require her team or her to sacrifice sick leave when they need it or the full parental leave they're entitled to. If she needs to adjust those goals or better manage her own bosses' expectations in order to relieve some amount of stress or suffering for her team, she'll try to find a way to do it.

Leaders can't tell our teams what they should do with their lives. But we should facilitate environments so that folks' life at work (or life at hobby, if appropriate for your leadership role) is not totally soul crushing.

This is hard. There are major structural reasons why work sucks. In every recent poll I could find from at least the last ten years, large majorities of American workers rate their jobs as mediocre or bad or similarly use language to describe their dissatisfaction with their workplaces.

In some ways, that's freeing for leadership. There's a lot that's out of our control, including but not limited to the financial realities of running a business or nonprofit combined with a government that wants to do the absolute bare minimum to create a social safety net and leaves much of what should be the welfare state to the discretion of employers.

So knowing all that, we can and should do everything in our power to accomplish our goals while making the day-to-day experience as minimally miserable as possible. Burnout doesn't have to be inevitable—there are things we can do as leaders to, if not avoid it entirely, at least stave it off for a while. And as a bonus, the things we do to make work more sustainable for our teams also make it more sustainable for us as long as we actually follow our own instructions.

Remote or flexible work is key, as we've already touched on. There's more, though: paid time off, vacation, and sabbatical policies, a four-day workweek, and family leave are near the top of the list. We've got to set up the policies and then take the rest ourselves.

• • •

This is going to be one of the most hypocritical sections I write because holy shit, am I bad at taking time off. Like so many workaholics, I'm not good at doing nothing—unplugging? Not looking at my email? Lounging around the apartment all day? Couldn't be me.

I intellectually, emotionally, and physically know this is bad. I came back from maternity leave with my first daughter in

March 2022 and didn't take my first real vacation from work until mid-July 2024—and even that my husband and therapist both had to gently force me into doing. This is not a brag; it's a shameful admission of failure. I am aggressively intentional at celebrating people who take time away from work (for whatever reason—vacation, being sick, caregiving, whatever) and really bad at actually doing it myself.

In the months leading up to that vacation, I could feel the effects of that extended work without rest—my temper was shorter, my exhaustion was more bone-deep. People would ask how I was feeling, and I'd say that I was eager for the physical trauma that comes with childbirth if it meant I could just get a break. (I was only kind of joking—2024 was a tough time to be a professional Democrat!)

It made me feel better to hear so many next-gen leaders identify a similar challenge with stepping back. Gillea Allison, the millennial publisher of *D* magazine, told me that "it stresses me out when I'm on vacation." Some folks pointed to work obligations that draw them back into their emails or crises that come up only they can solve. Others described an unbreakable addiction to work, to feeling needed, to feeling useful, to losing yourself in a project that distracts you from your "real" problems. So many folks named the same thing I struggle with: We really want people to take time off, but we exclude ourselves from that narrative.

Taking time off, both in short bursts and over longer periods of time, is one of the most prominent ways in which leaders can model good behavior for work-rest integration. So many of us struggle with it, in part because we feel like we got to this point as leaders due to our work ethic. We've absorbed #hustleculture and the need to #riseandgrind into our bones—we got here because, we tell ourselves, we were willing to outwork our peers. We're able to succeed as leaders because we're willing to do whatever it takes, putting our own personal needs aside if we must.

I'm telling myself this as much as I'm telling you: Our suffering has no greater purpose. Our teams would have every right to be bitter if we tell them to take vacation but don't take it ourselves because our actions speak louder than words. We've got to show them it's okay to step away from time to time, and we've got to build resilient systems that can handle an absence now and again.

Vacations don't have to be weeks on end. Ilana Glazer, the millennial comedian and activist you heard from in part one, described the small-but-meaningful decision to turn her phone off for Shabbat—from Friday sundown to Saturday sundown—as an "extremely impactful mode of rest" for her. Structurally, she tries to set it up for her team so that everyone has at least one week off every three months. If this works for you or is within your sphere of influence, consider implementing it.

Another option: Make vacation less stressful by ensuring you're not missing anything when you take it and simply shutting everything down. Take a look at the calendar and align your team activity with when people are already requesting vacation days. How much work is really getting done the week of July 4—can you close down that entire week and give people a summer break? How about the week between Christmas and New Year's—do you really need to be fully operational?

The answer might genuinely be yes. But also it might be no if only you had a little bit of time to plan for the closure, create some in-case-of-emergency response plans, or have a skeleton staff on call. You won't come back to the inbox from hell if there's no one at the office sending emails to begin with.

And yet another option: Your time off can also be longer! Run for Something has a sabbatical policy we're proud of: After working for the organization for three years, you can take up to a month off. Each additional year you've been with the organization adds another week to your sabbatical allowance. My cofounder, millennial Ross Morales Rocketto, took a six-week sabbatical in the summer of 2023. "Sabbaticals are great, A plus," he said, reflecting on the experience. "I don't think I would have made it through 2024 without that time." Stepping away from his leadership role gave him the space and time to think through what he wanted his future to look like and reenergized him for the work. Our policy is good, but in an ideal world, a sabbatical policy might be "three months off, once every five years," he suggested because the more time away, the more you can genuinely unplug and come back ready.

If you're not sure your organization can handle people being out of the office for longer stretches, consider it as a retention tool. Great people will stick with a team if they know they get a break. You should also reconsider your staffing structure because you should be ready to have people taking comparable lengths of time out for family leave (which we'll get to in just a few pages).

First, let's get into the ultimate solve for needing a break and the only reason I've been able to go this long without a true vacation: the four-day workweek.

• • •

Four-day workweeks (4DWW) are (1) the future and (2) an incredible tool to make work sustainable for you and your team.

As of this writing, there are at least several hundred companies and some public sector organizations in the United States who've adopted a 4DWW—A comprehensive study from 2025 across 2,896 employees in six countries found that burnout decreased by 71 percent, job satisfaction increased significantly, and 90 percent of the 141 companies involved made the policy permanent. Studies have also shown that organizations that trialed a four-day work week overwhelmingly chose to continue it.

Approximately 15 percent of US companies now offer some form of a four-day work week—a 300 percent increase from 2019 levels—and experts project that share will reach 25 precent by the end of 2026.[1] There have been congressional hearings on four-day workweeks and even some legislation introduced (albeit not yet passed) that would formalize the schedule nationwide.

There are certainly people who say it cannot be done for their specific workplace or their industry. Even in politics: It'd be hard for a presidential campaign to implement a four-day workweek when there's truly a hard limit on how long they have to get things done before Election Day. That being said, it is possible in more places and spaces than you'd initially think—organizations as varied as public schools, logistics companies, and tech firms have implemented the thirty-two-ish-hour workweek in various formats.

Run for Something implemented a four-day workweek after a pilot period in 2022. We got there slowly but intentionally.

First, in summer 2019, we tested out summer Fridays, a relatively common piece of many corporate cultures, where Fridays ended at 2:00 p.m. between Memorial Day and Labor Day—we combined that with a broader "no internal meetings before noon on Mondays" in order to give people space to get back into the week without feeling overscheduled. There were no major issues, so we decided we'd continue summer Fridays the following year.

Then in 2020, when COVID hit, things shut down, and people started feeling burned out really quickly—tempers were short, patience was thin, and no one was their best self. We decided to start summer Fridays early, kicking them off in April with no official end date. Again, no issues arose, so we kept the shortened Friday hours into the fall, winter, and into 2021.

At that point, Ross and I started wondering: What if instead of no work on Friday afternoons, we did no work on Fridays at all? We were tired, our team was tired, and shit still felt bleak. So we asked our incredible chief operating officer, Cassandra Gaddo, to look into the research and come up with a plan for testing this out. She ultimately found us a pilot to enroll in, where we'd test out the new schedule along with a bunch of global companies and a team of academics would regularly do surveys of our staff as to whether it was improving key metrics, like productivity, engagement, burnout, and anxiety. We polled our staff before we agreed, and while a majority gave an enthusiastic yes, some were concerned about whether they'd have the time necessary to get stuff done.

We started the new schedule on January 31, 2022, with the plan of testing it out for six months to see how it would go. Our team would simply be fully off on Fridays—no emails, no Slack, no Zooms, just a three-day weekend every single weekend. (And when holidays rolled around, sometimes that'd mean a four-day weekend.)

We put out a Medium post explaining our decision, tying it back to our organization's values. I expected some pushback from donors or partners—our work is urgent and (I believe) necessary to save democracy. However it is not an emergency room, nor are we first responders; we're not literally saving lives. And one of my strongest-held positions, as noted, is that while our mission is urgent, not every task in service of that mission is urgent—a 4DWW would force us to be ruthless in prioritization, rigorous about our time management, and able to discern the distinction between work that was useful and work that made us feel useful.

The first six or eight weeks were admittedly a little rocky. For anyone considering starting it themselves, as well as when talking to folks onboarding to our team, I am very up-front: You have to adjust to a new pace of work, a new way of scheduling yourself, a new vision for how long things may take or what your days will look like.

For people involved in a lot of cross-team collaboration work, days can feel jam-packed with meetings as you try to squeeze everything in. It takes a while to rebalance yourself and question: Does this need to be a meeting in the first place?

By the end of the pilot, however, our staff survey results were indisputable. Every metric you'd want to see go up (engagement, sense of balance, productivity, job satisfaction, etc.) went up, and all the bad things, like anxiety, burnout, and exhaustion, went down. Our overall output did not change (in fact, 2022 was one of our most impactful years to date), and our team was happy. Every job we posted once we transitioned to a 4DWW was getting hundreds and sometimes thousands of applicants.

Applicants and even new employees would ask: Do you all take it seriously? The answer is a hard yes. We treat Fridays like weekends. And just like in most jobs, most of the time, the expectation is that weekends are yours—you can plan to be free, and the time is to do with what you'd like. As a leader, very occasionally, I might schedule a donor call or chat with a reporter on deadline on a Friday afternoon, but those were few and far between and never anything internal. If I chose to deal with emails, I'd schedule them to be sent on Monday. If an event or trip required me to travel on Friday, so be it, but that happens on weekends or weeknights occasionally, too.

Two years into a 4DWW, I don't plan to ever work Fridays again if I can help it. Now as a parent, I have the luck and privilege of a four-day workweek but five days of childcare, which means Fridays have been reserved for errands, doctor's appointments, exercise, watching *Grey's Anatomy*, and cleaning up my apartment. I can go into Saturday with my family feeling well rested and ready to do all the things little kids require. The only reason this book exists is because I was able to spend nearly every Friday of 2024 doing interviews and writing—very little of it got done Monday through Thursday during normal working hours.

Working a 4DWW has made me a better leader, a better parent, a better partner, and a better person. It has made some day-to-day things harder, for sure, especially as it relates to scheduling, but ultimately I would not trade it for anything.

One of my employees who was most wary about kicking it off said after the pilot: "The things I have to say no to at work are balanced by the things I get to say yes to outside of it." After all, they get to volunteer in their kid's classroom on Fridays without hesitation.

A full 77 percent of US workers have said a 4DWW would have a positive impact on their well-being, including 46 percent who said it would have an "extremely positive" effect.[2]

If you're considering it, here are a few things to know going into it:

The transition will be hard. Treat it like any other onboarding time—the first month you'll feel stressed or like your head is underwater. The second month you'll start to get the hang of it. By the end of the third month, you'll never want to go back to the old way of doing things.

Outside stakeholders will be more understanding than you'd think. Mostly they'll just be jealous.

If you really don't think your team or industry can make it work, think expansively. If you can't have everyone take Fridays off, how can you restructure your team's workloads or schedules so there's full coverage without full staffing? Think about the time that gets killed in the middle of the day, reading viral articles in *New York* magazine or online shopping—what happens when that slack time gets refocused and punted to a single day?

If you really can't do it, keep the door open to other solutions. Can you try for no-meeting Fridays or no-email Fridays? Free yourself from the forty-hour workweek structure that's been around since 1940— literally, it's older than the boomers themselves—and be open to creative thinking. If you think, "Oh, everyone on my staff can do a 4DWW, but as the boss, I definitely can't," think again. If you don't take it seriously, they won't, either. You have to practice what you preach on this.

Finally, both a feature and a bug of the 4DWW is that it makes it incredibly easy to recruit great talent and really hard to get folks who are otherwise unhappy to leave their jobs. We've had much lower than expected attrition, which is great, but there are certainly some folks who probably would've moved on if we didn't have the structure we did.

Consider changing your schedule and giving your team the guardrails to be full people outside of work. It could be the best thing you do for yourself, your team, and your bottom line.

* * *

Another huge issue for next-gen leaders (and all people, really) as it relates to work-life integration is family leave.

Millennials and Gen Zers are having kids later in life (if we're having them at all), which for many of us is coinciding with the moment our generations are taking over leadership roles. In additional bonus challenges, many of us may be taking on caregiving responsibilities for aging parents or relatives. So whether it's for new babies in diapers or old relatives (also maybe in diapers), we're going to have to collectively figure out how to be in charge while also making the time to step away for our families.

No duh here: The lack of universal paid family leave is a huge problem in America. So many parents, especially women, have had to cobble together support from a mix of employer policies, sporadic state-based programs, and more (if they can access it at all). As a society, we *have* to fix this.

And: This is personally complicated for those in leadership roles. Veronica Tessler, millennial small business owner of a frozen yogurt shop in Iowa, got emotional when telling me about her inability to take leave after her daughter was born. She couldn't find many people in her community or network who'd similarly been a small business owner and a new mom at the same time but still, she tried to set herself up for success by off-loading some core parts of her workload to a vendor who ultimately failed her. "Forty-eight hours after my daughter was born, I was back to work—after an emergency C-section," she said, reflecting on the deeply painful experience. "I went back to work in the store less than two weeks after she was born to check on things."

That story is too common for too many new parents. Even for those of us fortunate to have paid leave, there isn't enough of a clear playbook on how to actually take the time. I didn't quite realize how messy this would be until I had my first daughter.

Early on, Run for Something established a family leave policy that included twelve weeks fully paid. We'd had one team member take leave over the years but not since the organization had dramatically scaled in size—so when I got pregnant with my oldest daughter in 2022, I began preparing for my maternity leave with the knowledge that how I did it would set the tone for how all current and future employees would think about their ability to access leave for themselves.

I scoured the internet for advice on how to set up a leave plan—it's not as simple as "hand off this project to that teammate" and "call this person for that question" when the projects are things like "raise all the money, speak publicly on behalf of the organization, think long-term about where we're going and how we're going to get there, and solve crises as they arise."

Everything I found online was either (sadly) guides on how to convince your boss or HR department you deserve paid family leave or how to write a coverage plan to give to your boss. There was little out there about how to take leave if you were already the boss and even less about how to prepare myself and my team for my eventual reentry.

I found a few peers who'd been in my shoes: top leaders who also became new parents while they were in the big job. Almost all of them implored: Take the leave! "I wish I'd actually logged off," one said to me, explaining even as she ran her own company and maybe could have (or should have) taken the time, she felt compelled to be back at work within a few weeks of delivery. Another explained how she was half-in, half-out during her maternity leave and ultimately found it more challenging (and frustrating!) both for herself and for her team than helpful.

I wanted to do it right! I wanted to take the time—for myself, for my growing family, and to show my team that we meant it when we said we had a leave policy. Also, like all benefits, the paid leave was literally part of my compensation.

So I had to make it up myself. I wrote memos, articulated out decision trees for who would make the call on which topic, and was fortunate to be able to tag in my cofounder on most of the big stuff that would fall on my plate, along with amazing members of our executive team.

Versha Sharma, millennial editor in chief of *Teen Vogue*, experienced the same challenges when she had her daughter. There hadn't been a *Teen Vogue* editor in chief who'd had a baby on the job in decades. Versha said she struggled hard with both her guilt and the practicalities because she didn't have a clear road map on how to set it up. She consulted with a number of senior women leaders who'd had babies on the job (or, in some cases, had had their babies decades ago), most of whom pushed her to take the time she needed.

Versha, like me, had a professional partner: her executive editor—a position that reported to Versha—had had a baby right before she did. They overlapped at work for barely three weeks before Versha went on leave, which was both so helpful because once Versha's daughter was born, her team "knew exactly what I was experiencing postpartum," Versha said, but also so stressful! Back-to-back leadership transitions meant everyone had to really lean on the systems and relationships they'd built over time.

So here's what you do if you're the boss preparing to take leave for any reason—and what to do to be a good boss for someone taking leave:

If this is within your control, ensure your company has policies that support paid family leave. This is not always possible depending on your role, but if it is, make it happen. If you need to advocate to HR, take on the fight. If you need to argue with a board of directors, make the case. There are countless resources online about how providing paid leave benefits to both the company and the employee is undeniably net positive. Ideally you should do this before you have to avail yourself of this policy, but if you have to be the first to push the limits, go forth and know that caregivers everywhere have your back.

Now, let's be real here: The actual problem is that family leave should not be a problem for individuals to solve. Tori Dunlap, millennial founder of a feminist financial-literacy company who you met earlier, expressed extraordinary frustration at the limits of what she was able to do. "I'm happy to pay for this," she said, "but in no other country am I, as a small business owner, even required to pay for this." She wishes she could afford to give everybody a year off, but "we're not at a level of revenue where I can pay for somebody to go out and pay for the replacement. That's just really tough."

She tries to live her values—her company's policy includes as much paid family leave as she can reasonably afford—but the onus shouldn't be on her to solve for a structural fuckup. Much like with childcare: This should be solved by the government, not by corporations! Become a care voter! And until it is: Do whatever you can to ensure that your company provides generous paid leave for caregivers.

If you're preparing for a new member of your family or for taking on caregiving responsibilities in some way: Actually take the leave. Every piece of research known to mankind shows that taking parental leave in particular is better for families, better for parents (both birthing and otherwise), and better for companies because losing employees who leave for companies with better family leave policies is extremely expensive in the long term.

If you have caregiving obligations—maybe an aging relative or a sick family member—that require your full-time attention, don't fool yourself. Trying to do it all is not going to work for anyone; you'll be both a bad caregiver and a bad leader in the process. Take the leave. As always, I want to call myself in here: My second maternity leave began a few weeks before the 2024 presidential election, so I came back to work for two weeks around Election Day, first to deal with the aftermath of the results and then to, sadly, do notifications around an organizational restructure. I never fully checked out, even if that was my intention. I struggled a lot with what kind of example this set for my team, along with the compounding bad feelings around the election and general postpartum malaise. It was not the best! But still: Be better than me.

If you're wary of it, or have a member of your team who is wary about it, or anyone is under the impression they're irreplaceable, start by making a plan. Start a running list—I just kept one in my Notes app—of all the things that made up a month of work: meetings you ran, documents you reviewed, decisions you made, crises that came up you had to solve, and silly things like, whoops, turns out your cell phone was set up as the two-factor authentication for a particular social media platform, or you're the only one who was authorized to call American Express and add new users to the credit card account.

This is a useful exercise both for preparing for leave but also more broadly for auditing how you as a leader are spending your time and whether or not you're *actually* the best person to be tackling a particular project.

Once that list feels exhaustive, do some sorting. Which decisions could be categorized by expertise needed? Which tasks need to be handed off or sorted out now, before you go out? Whom would you need to provide context to in order to make certain decisions and who should they be consulting when they do so?

You'll end up with various buckets of work, perhaps including categories like strategic decision-making, HR issues, external and internal communications, and more. Then each bucket—and sometimes each individual item within the bucket—gets a new owner, along with relevant documentation or context necessary for that person to take on the work.

One example from my leave plan: I've written a weekly email to a few thousand people (mostly donors and political partners) since the organization started. I do it myself, both because I like writing and because it's a helpful practice for me to ground myself in the stories of our candidates, frame the narrative for our community both internally and externally, and stay relevant in people's inboxes/minds.

In order to tag one of my excellent executive-team members on that project, I needed to brain dump with him on how I thought about that community and the goal of that email, share the way I gathered information for it, articulate the things I cared about including in the email (and the things I didn't), and mechanically, set him up with a log-in to the system that would allow him to send the email each week. Mentally, this was a lot of work—practically, it was about fifteen minutes total.

Do this for every single project. In addition, lay out what things you want to be called in on. Keep your list small, but consider including things like: (1) a serious personnel issue with one of your direct reports, (2) a financial problem that would have meant immediate structural changes to the organization, (3) a lawsuit, or again, an example from my list, (4) a headline or story about us bad enough in a big enough outlet that would have my grandma calling me asking me what's happening at work and if everything's okay.

Finally, while you should obviously prepare an out-of-office message, if you can, tag in someone to fully monitor your email inbox. If you have an assistant, great. If not, pick someone on your team you can trust and empower with internal materials. They should be responsible for keeping an eye on anything incoming that should be forwarded to someone else for response or forwarded to your personal email that absolutely must be reviewed before your return. This person should also have permission to call or text you if your attention is necessary.

This kind of rigorous prep will be exhausting. But it will give you the space to actually step away. I found a silver lining of all this is that it allowed me to hand off all kinds of things that probably shouldn't have been mine to begin with and to have some advanced thought into what would happen in the case of an emergency. In retrospect, I'm glad I spent as much time as I did on this process, and I'm glad I was wrapped up with the prep about a month before my due date, since, surprise, both my daughters were born three weeks early.

Prepare for reentry. As part of your leave prep, ask someone to keep running lists of what you'll need to review upon your return, along with any emails that you absolutely need to see and big updates you might miss. Schedule time a few weeks before you come back to clarify where you're at with your scheduling preferences—when do you want your days to start, travel restrictions, any accommodations you might need, etc.

On your actual first few days back, if you can, keep your schedule light. Reenter your inbox gently and review the documents prepared for you, and if relevant, debrief with the appropriate top staff. From there, schedule one-on-ones with each team member—over the next month, reenter the working world on your terms, gently and with grace for the new person you are.

If you're preparing to manage someone coming back from leave, you may feel similarly a little lost.

Jessica Post, millennial former president of the Democratic Legislative Campaign Committee, had her daughter a few months after I had my first. She told me how she had experienced the same issue both in prepping for her leave and in prepping for a direct report's leave: "I was googling how to be a good employer and how to support an employee's transition back into the organization—the only thing I could find was legal guidelines for employers and advice on how to bring up your maternity leave to your employer without losing your job."

We agreed—the most important thing you can do as a leader is be flexible. Coming from family leave is a real mind fuck. I left in November one kind of person and came back in March with a different body, different brain chemistry, and an entirely transformed list of priorities. The travel and events I would have been an absolute hard yes to before parenthood turned into hard conversations about what was worth my time and attention, knowing that each absence came with a different kind of cost.

Ross and I went into this process knowing that, when I came back, I might need different hours or modified support systems. As other members of our team have taken leave, we've created processes for them to block out time for pumping breast milk, doing childcare drop-off, or working modified schedules to accommodate other caregiving responsibilities.

For Versha of *Teen Vogue*, returning to work was harder than taking the leave. "It hit me—I had the intense guilt and the feeling that I just wanted to be at home with my baby," she said, "but I love my job, and I think my work is so important." She got hit with a wave of postpartum depression and anxiety—she didn't realize how bad it was until she was quite nearly too depressed to use the floor tickets she had bought herself for the Beyoncé Renaissance tour. "[My executive editor], the other new mom, was like: You have floor seats and you're about to stay home? You are *depressed* depressed." Versha ultimately got the mental health support she needed and the help she needed at work to find a balance between her daughter at home and her obligations at the office.

And modeling that paid off. Since her daughter was born, multiple other members of the *Teen Vogue* team have had kids—Versha is so proud she's able to lead a team that "intimately understands what new mothers, working mothers, and working parents face." Stepping back, all of this may seem ridiculous or privileged in the context of a country where, as of 2025, not even a third of private sector workers have access to paid family leave, and the United States remains the only OECD-member country without a national paid-leave policy. But that's why the onus is on us to both provide leave and take it ourselves. I can't find data on this, so take it with a grain of salt, but I would venture a guess that many of the companies that do not have paid leave policies are coincidentally run by leaders who've never felt they should or could take time off themselves. (I have often heard older men make the case that there was no reason for dads to take paternity leave. I wonder if their partners or kids would agree!)

That's why I think it's worth being idealistic, and encourage you to fight for then model generous leave policies. None of this is easy (especially in the context of a society that doesn't seem to care about parents) and often requires compromise. But in service of being a compassionate leader, a good parent, and a good person, it's worth doing as part of a larger system of guardrails so everyone—you *and* your team—can inch ever closer to balancing all the competing demands on our time.

• • •

Your job as a team leader is to create the space for people to get their job done, accomplish their goals, and not be miserable doing it. You need to be on the level about what you can and can't provide as a leader, what success looks like, what kind of behavior will and will not be tolerated, and where your boundaries are.

This requires a lot of work. It sucks. It will sometimes feel like process-process bullshit. You will be constantly defining things, then redefining them, and then repeating your definitions because people won't hear them or won't want to hear them.

You will fail. No matter how much good you try to do, someone will be disappointed or furious. No matter how much you let people have the space they need to be real people outside of their obligations to you and your team, some of them will feel like you are asking too much of them. Others will fail to meet your expectations, no matter how clear you make them, and you will have to make hard decisions.

You cannot please them all. All you can do is create sufficient guardrails for your team so they have the space they need to do their work successfully and still be full humans.

When you do this, you're giving people what they really want: control (within reason)—they have some amount of agency over where they're working, when they're working, and what they're working on.

Just as you defined yourself, you're doing the same for the organization: Stake out the boundaries of what your organization deems acceptable and requires in order to accomplish your goals, communicate those boundaries to your team, model them yourself, and hold to them. People can opt in or opt out of your team structure as they see fit, as long as they know their options.

This requires incredible amounts of work and thought, but here's the positive spin to all of this: What's good for your team is also good for you. If your team is working a four-day workweek, that means you need to, too, because you need to model good behavior. If you are providing the kinds of benefits that attract high talent, you get access to them, too. If you're creating an inclusive environment, that means you're welcome just as much as anyone else.

And most important: You don't succeed unless your team succeeds. If you want to do a good job and get the work done, you need to make sure your team has every possible resource (whether that's financial or in the form of time, tools, or psychological safety) to do it. Creating a good workplace for *everyone*—not just you or the top of the pyramid—is in your best interest.

When you skimp on benefits or decide to run people through the ringer for short-term gains, you're bringing on some longer-term pain. It may be cheaper, faster, or more efficient today to pay people less, or give fewer days off, or not spend time on management training, but consider what the cost of that over time might be.

If you burn through team members at warp speed, or have high turnover, or have managers who can't actually manage, you might get by for a few months, but you can't Band-Aid your way into long-term success.

So much of shitty workplace and leadership behavior tends to stem from someone thinking, whether consciously or not, "Well, I went through hell and survived, so they should go through hell, too." Consider all the people who already paid off their student loans who think the "kids" should stop complaining and put up the money, too.

You may have had to work eighty- or hundred-hour weeks, or survive abusive leadership, or get professionally hazed in order to get to where you are. If so, I'm so sorry. But don't assume that just because it seemed to help you (or at least not harm you) that it had to be done that way. That misery does not need to be passed on. One of my top-five favorite things about next-gen leaders: We are trying to break the cycle, and everyone benefits from that.

TRANSPARENCY: CAN YOU BE TOO HONEST?

As a leader, you have to show your work, let people see behind the curtain, work in the (not literal) nude—whatever metaphor you prefer. To do so, we have to think carefully about communication, expectation setting, feedback, and even (annoyingly) communicating about how we communicate.

Transparency is both one of the loftiest things to value and one of the hardest things to operationalize. But it came up in so many of my conversations with next-generation leaders. I'd ask folks to describe their leadership style to me using their own words, and an overwhelming majority of leaders use some variation of "transparent" in their response. Ashley Lynn Priore, a Gen Z chess champion and nonprofit founder, explained it as "everyone has an understanding of whatever values I'm bringing to the table because my values influence the decisions I make."

Jace Woodrum, the executive director of the ACLU of South Carolina, talked about wanting "people to know how I'm thinking about things and give them the opportunity to weigh in far before something is considered fully baked."

Allison Byers, a millennial tech founder and investor, connected transparency to trust: "It doesn't mean you have to tell everyone all the things all the time, but you do share important information. . . . It leads to that sense of trust."

All were essentially describing the same MO that is a defining characteristic of next-gen leadership: You have to ensure that everyone has the same clear understanding of what to do, why, and what success looks like.

This move toward transparent leadership is partially a by-product of the changing communication landscape of the last decade: We are drowning in content. It's not unusual for someone to be getting text messages, app notifications, news feeds, For You Pages, emails, Slack alerts, DMs, and occasionally the dreaded phone call, all of which are happening all the damn time.

An increase in supply tends to lead to an increase in demand: More information available means we expect more information. For consumers, that shows up through implicit and explicit requests to know more about things like supply chains, material sourcing, and sustainability measures. Think of how companies show soup to nuts how their clothes are made or exactly what each item costs in order to come at the end price.

At work, that looks like increasing demands to know who's making which decisions and why. After all, we can now find reviews online of what it's like to work somewhere; we can watch day-in-the-life videos of people working at all kinds of companies (and experiencing all kinds of bullshit) from around the world. We can see clips of people getting laid off or quitting their jobs that then go viral as bosses forget that nothing is ever off the grid anymore. One person can post on social media and tag a CEO, which can become ten people, which can become hundreds or thousands or more, and all of a sudden a CEO has to answer questions to stakeholders (or people who fancy themselves stakeholders) both internally and externally that they weren't necessarily ready for.

Teams have come to expect that day-to-day professional environments function like the rest of their lives, where one can look up the answer to nearly any question at any time. This is especially true of Gen Z teams, according to researchers Megan Gerhardt, Josephine Nachemson-Ekwall, and Brandon Fogel, who wrote about managing multigenerational teams in *Gentelligence: The Revolutionary Approach to Leading an Intergenerational Workforce.*

The push for transparency at work is also driven from the top by a desire on behalf of leadership to do things differently than many of us experienced when we asked previous leaders, or even, ahem, parents, to explain things to us. The answer, implied or explicit, was often simply: "Because I said so."

"Because I said so" is no longer a satisfactory answer for our teams who, when they don't have the requisite context, fill in a narrative for themselves that is often way less generous and way more negative than the reality. It doesn't always stick, but I like to say during onboarding: If you feel like you're out of the loop, don't assume it's intentional. The most likely answer is there is no loop to begin with. But ask!

More important, "because I said so" doesn't serve our goals. Intentional or oblivious obfuscation ultimately forces leaders into either being micromanagers or being deeply disappointed because teams did not meet the expectations that were never made explicit.

Transparent leadership in the age of remote work can be particularly tricky, especially with the constant threat of being recorded, and a workforce that demands to know "Why??" at every step.

So we're going to talk about why and how to "say the thing" when it comes to work. We'll identify some of the challenges and dangers of transparency that may make you hesitant and how to solve them and walk through an example of how to do transparency in a single instance that can serve you moving forward. Finally, we'll look at how, perhaps counterintuitively, focusing on the journey can ultimately lead you to the right destination.

* * *

Transparency is a core value for me and my organization, both internally and externally. This is in part because, when we started the organization, I was asking folks to donate their hard-earned money to what was simply an idea, and I felt better about that if I could be up-front about what they were giving money to. It's also because I'm a meh liar and a mediocre secret keeper—it simply felt much easier if everything was on the level so I didn't have to remember to whom I was saying what. If everyone knew nearly everything, problem solved!

Accordingly, our strategic plans are public every year, our top-line budgets are accessible and reviewed internally, we do regular all-staff meetings to reflect on key performance indicators—including programmatic and financial stats—and there are a number of ways staff have the ability to ask questions, interrogate decisions, and see what's happening. We have it baked into the way the organization operates. Outside of confidential HR discussions, there is very little that does not eventually come in front of the full team and, as appropriate, the public.

But as I've learned the hard way, there are challenges to transparency that, if not accounted for, can lead to complicated dynamics.

Stephanie Llanes, millennial managing director at a nonprofit whom you met earlier, reflected on one of the hardest things she's had to do as a leader: establishing a new process for hiring someone internally.

"Back in the day, it would have been automatically, 'We're going external,' to find someone," she said, but they wanted to try it differently. They opened up a hiring process with an application, a written assignment graded blindly, and then interviews, reflections on past performance, and ultimately a final decision. Lots of folks internally applied, and then "the person everyone didn't expect—because they were less experienced, newer to the team, etc., came out as the top runner" over others who had been at the organization longer. People were very upset in the aftermath.

"In an effort to be transparent and have a process everyone could participate in," Stephanie said, there was a ton of internal turmoil. "I don't know if doing the right thing is always the best thing," she said sadly, wondering if they should have gone external or just handpicked someone without running a rigorous process. Did that transparency actually serve its goals?

I've felt this tension myself, and many of the leaders I spoke with described similar situations. So let's be clear-eyed about what makes transparency so difficult in the first place and some of the ways to mitigate that up front.

Challenge: Giving people information often leads them to believe that they're entitled to give input on it, leading to decision-making processes becoming messy or annoying at best and disastrous at worst.

Solution: Ironically, one of the ways to solve the challenges of transparency is even more transparency—be explicit about what the decision-making process is, whose feedback is wanted, and whose isn't.

This can be hard on an emotional level because it can feel like you're disempowering folks from being heard or having a say.

This is where I remind you: That's a feature, not a bug. It is not everyone's job to be in charge. It's yours!

When you get explicit about who makes decisions and who gets to have input, you're also creating pathways for accountability, which is often scary, since accountability tends to be equated with punishment or consequences. But fear not because accountability is clarity, and next-gen leaders (and next-gen teammates) love clarity.

Looking back, I learned this intuitively when I was a teenager. I used to go absolutely bananas when my group of friends would sit and waffle for hours about what to do on a Friday or Saturday night.

"Someone just make a decision!" I'd beg, wishing for anyone to just step up and make the call as to whether we'd go to this party or that movie (but obviously not wanting to always be the one to make the decision myself). At some point, I lost my patience and just declared without precedent: Emily would be the decision-maker for the night, and whatever Emily decided, we would all go along with it. Deal? Deal. And much to my surprise, everyone agreed.

Decision-Maker™ became a core part of the way our friend group operated. We even wrote up rules, including specifics like I (Amanda) would always pick the decision-maker and whoever it was would make the call on the question at hand, no take backs. We included norms, like "being the decision-maker is an honor; treat it as such," and "declining the title is a dick move." The rules were typed and printed, signed by all members of the friend group, and laminated with Scotch tape, and we kept copies of them on hand. Even after we graduated high school, my friends would call or text me: "Here's who's at the dinner table. We can't decide what movie to see. Please name a decision-maker."

I had those rules in my wallet for years, a tangible reminder of how simply having clarity about how decisions would be made was a relief, even if the outcomes weren't always everyone's ideal. There was no confusion on process, no misunderstandings on who was accountable. This was a decision-making model in its crudest form.

I don't suggest implementing the exact same rules for your team. ("Dick move" is probably not appropriate language for your workplace.) But consider taking a cue from teenage-girl me—plus a variety of leadership books over the years—and create a shared language about decision-making and input. There are a number of models for decision-making that you can consider adapting, defining for your team, and then referencing as appropriate.[1]

1. **Command:** You make the decision entirely, without input from others. You're in charge. End of story.

2. **Release:** You delegate the decision entirely—when you do this, be precise about if you want to have any input or what kind of report back you want. Don't delegate and then try to claw back some kind of control; that's wildly annoying for your team and a bad use of your time.

3. **Consult:** Invite other people to influence you! You can gather ideas, evaluate options, make a decision, and then inform folks. Be clear in this model that at the end of the process, you are the decider.

4. **Vote:** This might be your impulse to lean on when you have tough decisions to make, but fair warning:

Only use voting as a tool when all the options are ones you're comfortable with and when the team will respect the final outcomes no matter what. Be clear what majority you're counting as a win: Do you need a simple majority of 50 percent plus one, two-thirds, or three-quarters approval? Is it a secret ballot or public? I love democracy as much as the next person, but in this context, it's not always the right answer.

5. **Consensus:** Like voting, you might be inclined to run decision-making by consensus because, at face value, it seems like the right call to build buy-in. Red flags abound: Operating by consensus is slow and hard and often denies accountability. Only use it when the issue is high stakes or supercomplex and when everyone must absolutely support the final choice.

6. **Metrics:** This is a little bit of a false model because what we decide to measure and prioritize is shaped by people. Data isn't a decision-maker; it's a tool for decision-making. But pointing to metrics up front in the process as the ultimate tool for shaping what's to come can be as clarifying as naming a person or model. (For example: If these specific metrics are *X*, then our next step will be *A*; if the metrics are *Y*, then our next step will be *B*.)

Defining and leaning on decision-making models can feel like an onerous process, and I'll admit, I haven't always been as rigorous about implementing them as I should have been—and I nearly always regret it later. But when I do, I'm always glad because it facilitates one of the most important principles of transparency: Not everyone necessarily likes the outcome, but everyone can understand how the outcome came to be.

Challenge: Sometimes people simply cannot handle all the information they want (or think they want). If you've established a precedent for being open, honest, and transparent, it can be really hard to pull it back.

Does everyone on your team know how to read a budget? Do they have the experience and context to understand how to balance short-term cash flow and long-term revenue projections? Do they have years of experience asking donors for money, knowing when a no is really a no and when it's actually a not yet? Does everyone have experience reviewing vendor contracts and knowing the ways to preempt the likely problems?

I'll answer my own rhetorical questions: No. Most of the time, they don't. And that's okay! It's not their job to also be an expert in 100 percent of everyone else's special skill sets.

But especially after a crisis or a break in trust in leadership, folks may clamor for more information as a way to assuage their own anxiety. You might encounter what I unaffectionately describe as "I gave the mouse a cookie, now they want the entire bakery, all the recipes, and also the job as head baker."

Said more kindly, you may end up in a situation where your team is demanding agency but without any of the commensurate accountability.

I'll speak from personal experience on this one: It feels bad all around.

Solution: You have to steel yourself to be disliked (which is, unfortunately, a significant part of leadership—sorry!) because sometimes the answer is simply no. It's not everyone's job to review every contract. It's not everyone's job to have line-item veto power over every decision the organization has made.

Repeat the mantra: Transparency is insight, not necessarily input.

As leaders, we have the experience necessary to see which problems are worth stressing over and which problems are par for the course. We are likely comfortable with some discomfort or ambiguity. Those beneath us in the org chart, especially the more junior folks, probably aren't, and that's okay. They aren't expected to be.

But depending on what we share and when, we might be introducing anxiety, worry, and a desperate cry for more information that they also won't understand.

One clear process point to help solve for some of this: creating and sustaining regular feedback loops, both on the individual and team-wide levels.

Feedback is usually understood to be (hopefully constructive) criticism, which is certainly part of the definition. I also like to remind our team that feedback can be positive! We should be regularly highlighting and celebrating accomplishments, both in one-on-one settings as well as group environments.

As a leader, you should be giving regular feedback in the way an individual likes to receive it, which is an explicit conversation you should have with folks as they onboard and then revisit once they get more comfortable.

There are approximately one million guides out there about how to give good, clear, specific, and action-oriented feedback, which have mostly stayed constant over the years, but the one thing to emphasize for next-gen leaders is that the expectation now is *immediate* feedback, both good and bad—think faves and RTs but for work products and behavior. "See something, say something" is shady and often racist advice for someone on public transit or at the airport but worthwhile to keep in mind when managing someone else's work.

The more relevant definition of feedback when it comes to transparency and level of access is spaces for teams to speak, to be and, most important, *feel* heard. Whether you use apps, Slack channels, surveys, informal office hours, one-on-ones and skip-level check-ins, or a different format entirely, create lots of opportunities for people to tell you what they're thinking and what they want.

When you can deliver and make changes based on that feedback, great—constantly remind people that you are doing what they asked. Literally:

> We heard from 79 percent of staff during office hours that they feel like the organization doesn't do enough to celebrate National Rescue Dog Day, a holiday which is obviously of utmost importance to many members of our team.
>
> We took that feedback seriously and have set up a Slack channel specifically to recognize rescue dogs among the team, will be highlighting team rescue dogs on our organization's social media platforms, and will be making a donation each year to a local rescue group. Thank you for giving your input!

Show that participating in the spaces to speak up is worth their time because, when you can, you'll try to deliver. And when you can't, explain why and, again, show gratitude for their time and willingness to engage. Close the loop:

> We heard from 79 percent of staff during office hours that they feel like the organization doesn't do enough to celebrate

> National Rescue Dog Day, a holiday which is obviously of utmost importance to many members of our team.
>
> Unfortunately, due to our work as a cat-loving company, engaging on National Rescue Dog Day would undermine our organization's brand. We absolutely hear you that this matters, so while we can't do anything publicly, we encourage you to share your rescue dogs internally and celebrate them on your personal social media.

It will feel like repeating yourself over and over again. You will disappoint people. It will suck and make you occasionally feel like you're going crazy. That's structural, not personal.

Challenge: Context collapse! Your Zoom calls can be recorded, your password-protected Google Docs can be downloaded or screenshot, your internal documents can become external viral content within a few minutes. A Slack or email you sent to three people on the team who know the backstory of a situation gets forwarded or ("accidentally") sent to someone else who has no or limited context, and all of a sudden you've got chaos on your hands, as information that would have previously been carefully managed through a communications cascade now hits audiences who don't have the benefit of background info.

Solution: On political campaigns, we used to say that you should assume any and all emails or written communications could end up on the front page of *The New York Times* and act accordingly. Obviously we didn't always take that kind of care, but there is a certain amount of thought that goes into what you put in writing when you've got that looming in the background.

I'm not saying you need to treat all communications like they could go viral at any moment—but you should assume that the email you're sending announcing a big launch or strategic shift internally will also go public. And if you think no one cares about what you do so why would anyone put it on the internet, well, if we've learned anything over the last few years it's that the internet's appetite for businesses and leaders to mock is insatiable, no matter the scale.

Don't let the fear of sunlight keep you in the shadows. To torture this metaphor: Yes, you might get sunburned. But with that comes warmth, vitamin D, an excuse for iced coffee, and much-needed trust among your teammates. Transparency, much like authenticity, must be used responsibly. It takes time, intentionality, and a lot of repeating yourself. But it is worth doing.

* * *

Two examples to learn from:

Millennial Jasper Wang is one of nineteen cofounders and co-owners of Defector Media, a collectively writer-owned, writer-operated media company showing a new model of ownership and leadership. Jasper came to them from a decade in management consulting, taking on the formal title of VP of revenue and operations but with the baked-in accountability of knowing that if two-thirds of the company voted to remove him, he'd be out of the job.

The organization is superflat in structure and supertransparent in ethos, and as of when we talked, they took zero outside investment. In addition to their roles as writers or editors, each member of the team takes on a role on at least one committee, from revenue to culture to PR, and takes ownership of different pieces of the company.

In the process, Jasper explained, they've come up with their norms and codes of conduct, redefining professionalism and revising as problems come up. Instead of the traditional media institutions where a few owners at the top rake in a ton of money (or, more commonly these days, a single billionaire owner or private-equity investors take over and run the outlet into the ground), everyone has a shared stake in the success and a shared responsibility for executing on it.

Jasper will fully admit: Their "communist collective of writers" can work because of the smaller size of the team, and he's unsure of whether it could scale. And there is inherent tension that arises as the core belief that everyone deserves protections in their job comes into conflict with the fundamental reality that not everyone is actually doing a good job. Everyone (or nearly everyone) is friends with one another, which makes the work environment deeply enjoyable and also can make it emotionally harder to hold people accountable. But the transparency—from how much they spend on software to how much every person makes—is an incredible step forward for media companies known for being shadowy about how their operations work.

Millennial Drew Miller took a similar approach to the software company he built, Base Two. He called his policy "semiradical transparency," which means a wide range of information—from salaries to strategic choices—is internally available, which "forces us to always think about perception of choices. You couldn't hide stuff." They build software for clients and aim to share as much as is safe with those clients, which lets them "build trust faster," he says. "When [clients] are like, 'Oh, they're just giving me their internals on the reason they're charging me what they're charging,' it forces us to be able to explain our profit margins."

Drew aims to treat people better than how he was previously treated in his bigger corporate roles at various software agencies. His perspective was that "policies can often become ends unto themselves, like dogma"—so his company tries to take strong positions but allow for persistent iteration over time. Drew explained that, eleven years into his business, almost every employee has altered a company-wide policy in some way.

His core belief is that to build the kind of organization that he wanted to work at, he needed to really care about people, think about them as humans, and never reduce them to numbers on a spreadsheet. Like Jasper, Drew questions whether "human empathy scales to ten thousand people," but he's willing to keep trying.

We've talked about this so far in mostly corporate environments, but transparency can apply to nearly any sector or enterprise. The best example of this came from millennial Marci Robles, who, when we spoke, had just left her job as a head coach for the women's crew team at a major university.

In Marci's first job as head coach over a decade earlier, she tried to just take the training program she'd experienced as an athlete and apply it to her team. It immediately backfired: They weren't training well, they were burning out, and they were completely lost in the mental aspect of the sport.

When she left that team and switched to being an assistant coach for a few years at a different university, she had a chance to observe a leader who thought carefully about not just the goals but the psychology of the athletes. "It was process based as opposed to goal based," she explained. "Prior to that, it had been: 'You've got to hit the score at the end of your workout.' Instead, he would give them starting goals like, 'This is the pace you're starting at,' and the kids were like, 'Well, what do we do with that?' And he'd tell them, 'Take it where you want it.'"

She gave context and then let them row from there. Her students had control over where they'd take the numbers—it opened up a level of risk-taking among the athletes as they'd push and hold back based on what they wanted and felt.

When Marci took a new job as head coach, she implemented the same kind of leadership and workout style. She said that while it took a bit for the athletes to trust her and to see that she wasn't going to yell at them if they didn't hit a specific number, ultimately a switch flipped. It moved from proving something to her to proving something to themselves. They were in charge of their progress.

In addition, Marci started explaining her decision-making process. She sat her team down in mandatory meetings and explained everything, from the training timeline to racing to community service. "I found if I left gaps in communication, then there was room for them to make assumptions."

She balanced the team's need for clarity about goals and the plan with her own need to be flexible, making promises to deliver week-by-week training and workout plans at the top of each week without committing to further-out specifics.

The final addition to her leadership style: She created a permission structure for her student athletes to take three mental health days a year. "It's so different from the kind of environment I grew up in as a student, where you just were expected to be able to manage it all," Marci said. But she could see her team needed it: A third of her team ended up taking at least one mental health day, and maybe a handful out of fifty students took all three. This has real impacts on the team—a nine-person boat missing even one rower has to do an entirely different kind of practice that day—but it was important for Marci to show her team that she had their backs. "This is a system that's in place," Marci explained, "this gives [the student] permission to say, 'I'm not okay.'"

The outcome of all those shifts: Her team won the conference championship for the first time. They had the trust, the skills, and the space—focusing on the process allowed them to successfully hit their goals, and everyone understood how and why they got there.

Consider what Ashley said in the introduction to this chapter: She ensures her team knows her values so they can understand how she approaches decision-making. They want to know how she's approaching her processes so they can trust her. That's a core part of responsible transparency.

Through the earlier chapter on responsible authenticity, you've got a framework for how you want your team to perceive you and what you're doing to tell that story consistently in every possible medium.

To apply the same lens of responsible transparency to the work product itself, you have to be clear about what you care about, what you don't, and why.

Say what success looks like, and say why it looks like that. Say what failure looks like, and why. Say who is responsible, when their deadline is, and what the consequences are if those expectations aren't met. Say it (and write it, and Slack it, and email it) over and over again. Say it, even and especially when it's hard and when people might hate you for it. There needs to be a shared language for why what you're doing matters. You need to all be working off the same dictionary.

Crucial Conversations, an excellent book worth reading if you're looking for specific tactical advice on having hard conversations both at work and outside of it, describes this all as "the Pool of Shared Meaning," which is "the birthplace of synergy."[2]

We have to give people as much context as possible, as early as possible, and give them a chance to ask questions, build on the process, and contribute to the metaphorical pool. We have to let them fill the pool with us, instead of just saying, "Dive in the pool; you'll like it."

We do this because it gets better results—literally, people need to know what success looks like. But beyond that, aggressively transparent communication is a core factor to building trust. Our teams need to believe that we're all working in the best interest of our mission, and to believe that, they need to know what *we* as a team and as individuals believe.

Let's work this through an example project—it could be a stakeholder memo, it could be a campaign launch, it could be competitive research, or a press release, or a social content calendar—it could simply be a plan for which family is in charge of bringing snacks to the kids' soccer games over the course of the season. The same theory applies regardless of the actual product.

Before you ask anyone to do literally anything for this project, get right with yourself first and be ready to lay out all the context you could possibly provide. A few questions to consider:

- Why do they need to do it? How does it connect to the larger team goals and objectives?

  Example: A snack calendar is important to ensure the kids all have something to eat after each soccer game. If they don't, they get grumpy—and one of the core goals of this soccer season is happy kids. Having clear, well-defined ownership of snack bringing will ensure that each family does their part and no one person is responsible for all the snacks, which would be counter to our efforts to build community through this team.

- What does it look like if they do it well? Do you have examples you can point to? Can you explain *why* success is what it is? What would it look like if they failed? Don't forget logistics.

Example: A good snack plan will include an outline for the entire season, labeling which family is responsible for bringing which snacks to which game, including location of each game if we know it and what time the game starts. It will include all known allergies for the kids on the team in a called-out section of *do not bring*: so there is no confusion about what is and isn't appropriate.

There will be detailed instructions on how much of each snack to bring, which other items are expected (e.g., napkins, cups, trash bags, etc.), and when to have it ready by, along with budget suggestions. There will also be a section on what to do if you're unable to make the assigned weekend game, which details a process for how to trade weekends or tag in backup in case of a sick kid.

A good snack plan will be a singular source of truth for all team parents on how snacks are operating this season. A bad snack plan will leave the first parent setting precedent based on their whims or capacity and everyone else feeling shitty about themselves if they can't live up to it.

The format should be a Google Doc, with commenting ability turned on for all parents.

- What is the deadline? Why is that the deadline?

  Example: The snack plan needs to be finalized at least three weeks before the games start, so parents can plan accordingly. It would be annoying but not the end of the world if the plan was not ready until two weeks before the games start; it would be rude and inconsiderate to deliver the plan any later than that.

- What will feedback look like? How will the person responsible be held accountable for their success or failure?

  Example: There will be a light process for the snack coordinator to solicit feedback on an initial draft. The soccer team has already gathered allergy info for kids, and the league has a suggested budget limit for snacks; the volunteer snack coordinator should put pen to paper on an outline (including suggestions for the types of snacks, the precedent they want to set for what is appropriate, and a framework for which parents are responsible when and for what) and circulate it via email to the team leadership committee ideally ten days but no later than one week before the final deadline for them to give feedback. The only person who must weigh in is the overall team coordinator; everyone else can look if they want to or have thoughts, but it's okay if they don't have time.

  Obviously we're not going to fire the volunteer snack coordinator. But if they don't deliver, the kids will go hungry, other parents will be pissed, and they won't be welcome back next year as part of the coordinating committee.

Especially early on in a working relationship, err on the side of overcommunication. Does this all feel really silly or intense for a snack outline for a soccer team? Sure. But also: If you're a first-time snack coordinator for your kid's soccer team, wouldn't you be grateful for this clarity on what your role entails and how to succeed at it? The instructions might feel overwhelming, but there would be no ambiguity.

At the bare minimum, you need to be crystal clear on four key points:

1. Who is the owner?

2. What are they doing?

3. What is the deadline for when they need to do it?

4. How will you follow up?

That fourth question is key: It's accountability. If you want people to feel accountable, you have to give them a chance to be held to account—that means you have to be a hard-ass when the situation calls for it. That also means you need to praise things when they're good.

Apply the same kind of framework to any project, big or small. How are you explaining your thought process? How are you showing your work? What information does your team need to know in order to succeed, and what else would they need to know in order to knock it out of the park? Beyond that, what *else* do they need to know in order to make the right decisions when things go beyond the scope of what you outlined?

This requires more work on your part. (There's a reason our parents and bosses used to say, "Because I told you so"—it was absolutely easier for them.) But as you go, the virtuous cycle builds on itself: You define success for your team, they deliver successfully because they know what good looks like, you celebrate them, and then the next time around you have to do a little less defining because everyone's already aligned, and so on and so forth. It's a lot of prework, but it pays off.

• • •

As leaders, it can sometimes feel like a waste of time to spend so much effort on explaining not just how the sausage gets made but why the sausage gets made that way—over the years, I've often found myself lightly irritated that we'll spend hours in meetings discussing our communications norms or drafting and then editing and reediting project plans when we could just be *doing the damn work*.

But I remind myself, and I'm reminding you: The journey is easier when everyone is aligned as to why you're on it in the first place *and* you can still reach the destination (and maybe hit some great rest stops along the way).

I look to politics for one of many examples on this. We've got an expression in campaigns: Only winning is winning.

This feels obvious—literally, only winning is winning! Winners in elections get to make policy, build majorities, shape the path forward. Getting 49.99 percent of the vote in a 50-percent-plus-one election simply doesn't cut it, no matter how close you get.

But multiple things can be true at the same time: Only winning is winning, but sometimes, depending on your goal, losing is also winning. In politics, this might look like cutting the margin of loss—taking what was previously a 70–30 election into a 60–40 or 55–45 election—that lays the groundwork for the subsequent election to be even closer and more competitive.

Next-gen leaders get this. We believe it isn't just what you accomplish but why you accomplish it and how you accomplish it that matters. It's no surprise this was one of the most common threads across nearly every one of my interviews, and it's one I see the most reflected among the thousands of next-gen leaders I've worked with and observed over the years.

On top of all the reasons discussed throughout this chapter, I suspect it also stems from one other factor: As basically every public poll over the last few years has shown, we absolutely don't trust institutions anymore, and we are slowly losing our trust in one another.

Per *The Atlantic*:

> In 1972, more than 45 percent of Americans said that most people are trustworthy. Since 2006, that number has been barely more than 30 percent. . . . In 2019, 73 percent of those under 30 agreed that "most of the time, people just look out for themselves," and almost as many said, "Most people would take advantage of you if they got the chance."[3]

Those numbers have only gotten worse. According to a spring 2025 survey from Pew, 44 percent of American adults say most people cannot be trusted.[1] As a society, we don't tend to believe anyone will actually do what they say. With the addition of AI-generated work, it becomes harder and harder to tell what came from someone's brain and what came from a robot. Next-gen leaders in particular are being forced or are expected to adopt this technology while still grappling with our own comfort with it. If you cannot trust your lying eyes, as the expression goes, who can you trust?

In our own ways, big and small, next-gen leaders are trying to solve for that. Whether we're leading at work, in government, in our communities, or on our local neighborhood sports teams, we're doing our part to carefully rebuild the social fabric and model a new way of operating that hopefully our institutions can take on, too. You might not realize it, but when you're transparent with your team, you're low-key saving democracy.

It's hard and scary. Showing how the sausage gets made can result in being yelled at (or worse) for how the sausage comes out. But we do it because we believe it matters—and just as important, it gets us better sausage at the end. Transparency is both a good value to hold in and of itself as well as a means to accomplishing our goals. It's a business imperative as much as a moral one. Consider it a win-win.

PART THREE

If the questions are . . .

How do I find community when I can't be friends with my employees, don't have many peers, and struggle to find a mentor?

How do I survive the pressure?

How do I practice self-care in a way that isn't bullshit?

The answer is:

By maintaining strong boundaries, armoring yourself with integrity, and finding an identity beyond your job.

HOW WE SURVIVE: FINDING COMMUNITY AND JOY

Heavy is the head that wears the crown, so they say. But for next-gen leaders, the crown has gotten exponentially heavier.

We're dealing with all the things we've talked about in parts one and two of this book so far: the emotional labor required to be yourself (but not too much), the rapidly shifting definitions of professionalism, the need to perform yourself online in the most strategic way possible, the changing demands of employees in the workplace, the perpetual rewriting of policies and procedures so people can be their real selves but not necessarily their full selves, the persistent requirement to explain your work in service of transparency, the limited number of concrete examples for all this, plus the work itself is usually pretty hard.

If you're at all like me or many of the leaders I talked to, you might wake up some days wondering why you took this role in the first place. You're alone, and it feels like there is always someone mad at you.

I want you to hear me loud and clear: The problem is (probably) not you. But as we'll talk about in this chapter, there are things you can do—finding community, steeling yourself to criticism, and practicing non-bullshit self-care—that can make it all at least a little bit easier.

The problem is that the thing you are trying to do is fundamentally isolating. Structurally, leadership is lonely. By definition, we are responsible for things few others are—the decisions that come to our desks are rarely easy and often have big consequences for others, whether that's about their livelihoods, their working conditions, or how intense spirit week at the elementary school will be. We exist in a state of vulnerability, as every decision and action opens us up to criticism or worse.

Admittedly, this is a hard thing to talk about because bosses are rarely sympathetic figures, and many bosses of yore have acted in a way that makes it hard to pity them. And there are indubitably perks of being in charge, including but not limited to money (if relevant to your leadership role), corner offices (LOL), power (kind of!), and occasionally fancy parties (which rarely have enough food).

But when we don't talk about the hard stuff, too, people assume that their leadership failures are personal. If no one else is feeling frustrated then it must be that you, the reader, are the only person not tough enough to cut it.

That's just not the case. You may feel lonely, but you are not alone.

In this chapter, we'll look at how relationships change with your team when you are the boss—including the challenges and benefits of hiring your friends or becoming friends with the people you hire, and how you should never, ever call your team your family.

Then we'll get into the mechanics of networking and community building among people in similar leadership roles and some specifics on how others have found their way into community. We'll examine some of the practical consequences of being the first or only to take power and walk through some concrete tips for finding mentors, sponsors, or alternatively, thought partners.

Alas, community is necessary, but it alone is not sufficient. You've got to mentally and emotionally steel yourself to get through the tough days. You need to cultivate the muscle of both protecting your peace and finding your joy, even amid the bullshit. So finally, we'll get into how to build your own protective armor in the form of your integrity and how to keep the haters from getting too loud.

* * *

Running a start-up involves a lot of hard moments. Over the years, Run for Something has been rejected from funding proposals, been a few weeks away from not being able to make payroll, dealt with personnel issues and negative press, and taken big swings that have failed.

But nothing was worse personally or professionally than the first time we had to do layoffs.

The year 2023 was incredibly hard for political fundraising—across the industry, my peers and I were struggling to raise the money we needed to do what we felt was democracy-saving work. While Run for Something had grown exponentially after major 2021 and 2022 success, our fundraising was not keeping pace. As we got close to the end of the year, we realized we were likely going to have to lay off some staff to get the budget to a place that felt sustainable for the long-term health of the organization.

Those last few months were some of the hardest yet. As we hustled to raise every last penny, ultimately bringing in half the year's total revenue in the final eight weeks, our executive-leadership team, in consultation with our board, began to consider what staff cuts we would need to make to reduce our overhead.

As we collected more data and made more specific decisions—things like the exact scope of budget cuts needed, the intended timing, the size of the severance packages we could afford, and more—the isolation that had been par for the course over the years became even more acute. There were no right answers, only bad and worse trade-offs. We had to think through every single step, from how to communicate that layoffs were happening without introducing unnecessary anxiety to logistics like literally turning off email access, handing off projects, and processing offboarding.

January was horrible. Nearly every night, I wept the kind of full-body sobs that leave you wrung out and thirsty. I rambled on and on to my ever-patient husband, to my therapist, and to myself, alone on the streets of New York, walking the dog in the crisp 6:00 a.m. air, wondering if it'd be easier to just shut the whole thing down. "I could just do something else—literally, anything," I'd say to myself. "It would surely be easier than this."

I stopped being able to sleep more than two to three hours at a time. I was literally sick to my stomach, feeling the bile rise in the back of my throat after every call on the topic. Per my Apple Watch, my heart rate shot up ten beats an hour or more during each meeting—"work as cardio," I'd bleakly joke to my cofounder, Ross.

Even writing this now, I feel my heart racing because no one wants to hear how hard layoffs are for the boss. As hard as they were for us, they were harder still for the employees we had to let go.

I do not want anyone's pity. We are not the sympathetic figures in this story. We are the ones who fucked up, failing to predict how dark the fundraising would get in 2023 and hiring faster than we could sustain. This was our mistake to own.

It's easy to dehumanize leaders, but as someone joked to me during a conversation about this book, bosses have feelings, too—and the week of the layoffs was the worst week of my career, including losing a presidential election I'd spent two years of my life trying to win. The months after were nearly as bad, as staff processed their feelings.

There is nothing I could've done that would have made that process any easier for me, nor would I necessarily have wanted it to be less painful. It should always be really hard when you're changing someone's economic conditions. It should always feel agonizing. I don't ever want to be inoculated against the weight of that power.

I have spent hours (days? weeks? what feels like years? what is likely to be the rest of my life?) thinking through every decision point, from the scale-up that began in 2022 through to the way we ran layoffs in 2024, and evaluated whether I would have made the same final decisions. And at every point, I feel confident the answer is yes. Given what I knew at the time, I would have grown the organization in the same way, and I would have run the layoff process in the same way. There are choices around the margins I might have done differently, but ultimately, I know I did the right thing for both the mission and the organization.

When I questioned why I stay in this role and at this organization, I re-centered that core idea: The mission matters. The work itself matters. I believe in what we are doing, even when it's hard. At the best moments, leading has been a privilege, a joy, and an honor—the conversations with staff who've told us this is the best place they've ever worked, the candidates who sent notes saying they wouldn't have run for office without us, the elected officials who take meaningful action to make life better for their communities and credit us with having their backs—it all makes it worth it.

When we made the news of our layoffs public with an honest and painful statement on social media, I heard from other leaders who'd been in my shoes or, sadly, were about to be. They affirmed for me how hard it was, how there was no right way to do what we had to do, and how difficult it had personally been for them. In ways big and small, their emails and texts reminded me that while I may have felt lonely, I was not alone.

It is the same feeling I sometimes get when I scroll social media in the middle of the night. There's an influencer I follow who does a lot of new-mom content. She often posts at 2:00 or 3:00 or 4:00 a.m. while feeding her infant, shouting out the other middle-of-the-night moms who are up with their babies. I often saw her content when I was up with my babies in those tough first few months.

It was hard, no question about it. But there was something comforting and even gratifying about knowing that all across the Eastern Seaboard, as I sat in my rocking chair equal parts grateful to be holding my healthy daughter in my arms and desperately wishing she'd go the fuck to sleep, there were other parents feeding and changing and soothing their babies, too, staring at the same moon (or same Instagram post). We were apart, but we were together, and in that way, we could deal with the literal and metaphorical shit.

Sometimes hard things are hard simply because *they are hard*, not because we are failures or incapable of meeting the moment. And when they are hard, we can't complain to our teams, we often don't have direct peers, and our friends who've never had to fire someone don't always get it.

So many of the folks I talked to identified loneliness as one of the most surprising and persistent parts of leadership. They explained how their relationships with their colleagues changed, how they felt isolated or how they had to intentionally isolate in order to make the hard decisions. Especially for those who are the first or only of their community to rise up the ranks, they didn't see others living and leading like they did.

While it is almost certainly true that leaders of all generations have felt lonely, for next-gen leaders, the solutions aren't as easy as just going to the strip club with the bros, hitting the golf course on a sunny Saturday, or networking at conferences and exchanging business cards. The way we think about and build community, both practically and philosophically, is different from the boomers that came before us.

Within our teams or workspaces, the flattening of communication tools mixed with the expectation that work provides the structure for our social lives elevates the complicated nature of being friends with the people you're leading. This gets even harder when divides between teams and leadership are formally defined or when legal guidelines get put in place about what can and can't be shared between different levels within an organization.

Additionally, the pandemic-forced pause of in-person networking combined with the transition to fully or partially remote work means we don't have the casual ability to form relationships with other leaders. Instead, we're leaning on technology and community structures that our grandparents (or old bosses) would find baffling or possibly unprofessional.

And on top of all that, so many of us have been advised for years to "find a mentor!" as a necessary part of our career growth.

But it's easier said than done and even harder to do when there simply aren't a ton of people like you who've been in your shoes.

But we can't let the challenges discourage us. As they say on one of our collective favorite early 2000s TV shows, *Lost*, we live together or die alone. (Also, don't open the hatch.) Our most valuable nonrenewable resource is our relationships with others—that includes our teams, our peers, and our support networks outside of our leadership roles because they give us a huge portion of our ability to withstand the bullshit.

Resilience—a necessary skill and trait for a leader—is often understood to be individualized. But as Soraya Chemaly puts it in her thoughtful and well-reported book *The Resilience Myth*, "we cope, change, survive, and thrive together, in interdependent, mutual caring relationships."[1] Even the toughest, roughest, most enduring leader only truly gets through the hard times with the help of others.

• • •

Elise Joshi, Gen Z executive director of Gen-Z for Change, a collective of progressive content creators, manages a team of around eighteen people, all between the ages of seventeen and twenty-six years old. She described her leadership style as "trust based and as friendly as you can be while managing someone's payroll."

Elise started out as the strategy director and became the ED about a year later. She explained that as the team has grown and professionalized, "I think I had to realize that as much as they are my friends, they're not my friends, and it's sad." She couldn't casually text on weekends or go out for drinks with people that she might have to give hard feedback to later. If she was struggling at work, she couldn't complain to the people she managed.

When she first took on the job of ED, the organization was more horizontal in structure, but as that changed, she said, "At the end of the day, I feel a huge burden: If I don't fundraise enough, then I have to let someone go. The mere fact that I have the ability to do that—and I want to do it equitably or fairly, but still—I'm the one in the position to do that" was isolating. "I'm not sharing all of me," she said, "because it becomes so much harder to give all of you, and have deep friendships with everyone on the team, and then also be a boss. I actually feel like that might make me worse [as a leader]."

This is the challenge that came up again and again in my conversations and has come up for me personally. You can and should be friendly with your team. But you simply can't be their friend because friendship is, at least by Plato's definition, a relationship between true equals. The power dynamics in a team environment are such that there is no equality, no matter how hard you try to pretend there is—and the first time you make that mistake unambiguously sucks.

Those uneven dynamics are particularly clear when you have to make hard decisions about someone's livelihood. Letting employees go—whether for financial reasons or performance-based issues—never gets easier, even when it's in service of your goals. A little bit of emotional distance can help keep you focused.

The truth of the matter is, if you can meaningfully affect someone's economic status in any way, they are not your friends, and unless they are literally your family (which comes with its own problems), they are not your family. "We're all friends here" or "This team is a family" is coded language that diminishes the actual transactional nature of the relationship and is often an excuse for harmful behavior or bad management.

That doesn't mean you don't care. You can care deeply about your team—send flowers when a loved one passes away, ask questions about their interests, even have careful social interactions—but you can't ever forget the boundaries you need to maintain. Having a strong responsibly authentic framework is helpful here; knowing what you share about yourself and what you don't is a way of modeling the kind of relationship you want your team to have with you and vice versa.

And I hope this goes without saying, but I'll say it anyway: Do not begin a romantic or sexual relationship with anyone you manage. I don't care if you think they're your soulmate. Even if you think you're meant to be, the chemistry is off the charts, you just can't resist it, how could anyone fight this love story, this is the happily-ever-after to end all happily-ever-afters—don't do it. You're opening a door to trouble of all kinds (legal, financial, emotional) that you can't close. If it's meant to be, it'll still be meant to be when you're no longer making decisions about that person's salary.

Being friends (or, god forbid, more) with your team can make it hard for you to always act in a way that's goal oriented, equitable, and fair. Emotional distance is hard to maintain, especially in high-stress environments, but you will rarely regret having kept your boundaries solid.

Now, I will note: There is a distinction between collaborating with your friends and directly managing your friends. If you have the chance to bring on someone as a peer that you are not responsible for, that can be a key way to mitigate the loneliness of leadership.

Millennial Sabrina Hersi Issa, a human rights technologist who is one of my role models when it comes to community building, noted that she felt strongly about working with her friends when possible because the inevitable conflict at work makes the friendship stronger *if and only if* you have good tools to navigate said conflict.

Sabrina said, quoting one of her best friends (who, she noted, was paraphrasing poet David Whyte): "Friendship is like committing to standing on a bridge of perpetual forgiveness. You're both agreeing to stay forgiving each other for as long as you both are standing on the bridge." She explained: Conflict either makes her relationship better or it collapses the relationship, and either way, that's clarifying.

I heard this from a number of the leaders I talked to: Working with friends requires intense self-awareness and confidence in the strength of the relationship but can be transformative when done right.

Gen Z congressman Maxwell Frost, who represents Orlando in the US House of Representatives, described his friendship with one of his teammates, Nya. "She's one of the smartest people I know," he said. "I want to do a lot of things—and always, for my entire life, I've had trouble prioritizing them and then also following through with every single one of them because there's so much that pops up," he explained. Nya is the opposite of that, the congressman said. "She'll be like, 'Okay, what about this, this, and that,'" gently pushing back on the feasibility of his ideas. "She's not saying it to talk me down or mess things up. She believes in it, and she wants to see it happen, and she knows that [pushing for specifics] is the way to make it happen."

Sami Sage, millennial cofounder of Betches, a women-focused media company, started her company with two friends she's known since she was ten years old. They grew up together, went to college together, and even lived together their senior year. "We always had our little projects," she said. "We started as a blog—a counterpoint to what was, at the time, a very toxic, fluffy, vanilla women's media." That blog became Betches, which became a full-fledged website, a book, a massive following across a network of accounts on Instagram, a collection of podcasts, and more.

Sami's the first to say her setup is unique—she and her cofounders are more sisters than friends; they've been there for one another for every iteration of their lives and their business. But when I pushed her for any hot tips for working with friends, she suggested three simple guidelines, which ring true both for working with friends and working with anyone:

1. Clearly delineate each of your lanes and responsibilities.

2. Have a mutual commitment to open communication so issues don't fester.

3. Trust will get you through the pain points.

I built Run for Something alongside Ross—we knew each other socially before we went into business together, but over the years we have become incredibly close. (Literally: He gave a toast at my wedding, was one of the first people I told about each of my pregnancies, and is my older daughter's godfather.) Not all cofounder relationships work well, but we have been incredibly lucky and also, to Sami's point, deeply deliberate about division of labor and who has what kind of decision-making power.

If you don't have to go it alone, don't. There are few if any arenas in life where you get a trophy for doing something the hard way.

• • •

Being genuine friends with your team is, in general, a no-no—but that doesn't mean you can't have friends. (Duh.) You have to build relationships with your peers, whether it's leaders at your level internally if you've got them or, even better, leaders who share your challenges but exist outside your workplace. That means everyone's least favorite word: networking.

For next-gen leaders, the tactics of networking have wildly shifted. Some of that is due to the pandemic, some of that is due to generational differences, and some of it is practicality: Many millennial and now Gen Z leaders are also caregivers in some way—either to our aging parents or our tiny kids—and our time is precious.

So we think differently about how to build community. Sometimes that's through formal organizations, sometimes that means group chats, sometimes that means through friendships that exist entirely through fave-ing someone else's Instagram stories. Here are a few tactics you could consider as you seek out relationships with other leaders.

Take it online: Kate Watson Moss, a millennial lawyer in Chicago who recently became a partner at her firm, described the way networking has changed for her generation of lawyers—"It used to be a lot of local groups," she said, mostly in person with events. "Now the biggest female-lawyer parent community is on Facebook. Ironically enough, this group is called Esquire Moms, and it is a humongous group. If I ever need to refer something out of my jurisdiction or out of my practice area, I just go there—I find the people that I have connected with there and have referred matters to are so much more on top of it."

For Kate and for so many other next-gen leaders, connecting online just feels natural. Kate referred to the Reddit group she joined when her son was born—she still keeps in touch with them and when we chatted, she had plans to visit one of them in Utah in the next year.

Some next-gen leaders referenced professional LISTSERVs that have been lifelines during career shifts, even as they've never met in person—others identified Instagram comment sections, Discord servers, or Slack channels as places they've found community. Geography is no longer a limiting factor to the career connections you can build—you can meet and build relationships with people in similar life circumstances from anywhere in the world. Some of those online spaces can feel kind of cheesy or a little too formalized for some folks' taste (read: me), but they can be unbelievably valuable for people who find the structure helpful.

There's also the reverse path of taking IRL relationships online. Krissy Wall, a millennial development executive in Hollywood, found herself starting what she called an "accidental networking group" among women who run production companies like hers after dinner with some friends who do similar jobs. They realized that none of them have peers at work they can consult with, so they casually but intentionally formalized their own space—a WhatsApp group with regular monthly get-togethers—that has few rules beyond that every member must have a specific kind of job and that it's intentionally all women. Krissy described the group chat and get-togethers as "like group therapy," where they talk about everything from confirming business-related rumors to commiserating about being working moms to the challenges that come with being women asking for money.

Group chats are a go-to for so many of the next-gen leaders I talked with. Ruwa Romman, a millennial state legislator in Georgia, found working in the chamber as a member of the minority party and as a young Muslim woman to be isolating until she got more intentional about it, setting up a Signal chat for some of the folks she'd worked with over the last ten years. Sometimes that space would be for professional coordination; other times it'd be for venting or just shooting the shit.

As long as everyone in the group chat understands the core principle of a group chat—if even one screenshot leaks to someone it shouldn't, there is opportunity for mutually assured destruction—you're in the clear. Just be on the level about what is and isn't appropriate for discussion and why.

Outside the ones with my friends and the many chats I'm in for various groupings of moms/parents, I've been in some networking group chats over the years—in particular, one for women who became executive directors unexpectedly and one for a few colleagues who do similar high-dollar fundraising—that have been invaluable. The ability to shoot out a quick text and ask an informal question or even just to see other people talking about a problem I've experienced has helped me feel less alone.

Write it all down: Sabrina, whom you met a few pages earlier, used to spend something like 70 percent of her year bouncing around the world advising and solving big, sticky global problems. To avoid being persistently lonely, she had to get rigorous about what she calls "intentional practices of connection." She started the practice when she became a caregiver for her father and other family members early in her twenties, forcing her to be more protective of her time while so many of her peers had the freedom to be more selfish: She couldn't just count on connections to happen without her being proactive about it. Now when she has trips on the books, she does what she calls a "trip build," writing out a list of the people she wants to see in any given city, and reaches out to make the time to see them. She literally keeps a list!

Similarly, Nikki Stokes-Thompson, millennial chief of staff at Ariel Alternatives, the private-equity subsidiary of Ariel Investments, the country's first Black-owned investment-management firm, is aggressive about networking, but not in the way some imagine it to look. "Conferences are not my favorite," she said, laughing. "My approach to networking is very tailored and very intimate." She explains: She literally writes things in the Notes app on her phone. "I leave a dinner with a client. I write down, 'He has two sons who are going to college next year.' These details are incredibly important to me as I get to know each person on a human level." And then the next time she sees him, she brings it up! She sees her relationships and connection building as her superpower—why not systematize it?

It feels tacky, obvious, or overtly transactional to literally keep lists and notes on people you want to know. But if it matters to you, write it down.

Join a board: Gillea Allison, whom you briefly met earlier, is the millennial president of a family-run media company in Texas. She feels the particular pressure of both being a boss and being part of the boss's family—she can't ever really turn it off around her colleagues. She built some peer networking groups among other second- and third-generation members of family businesses that she's found helpful over the years but said the actual place she's found value—perhaps surprisingly—has been nonprofit boards.

"It's a different level of relationship," she explained, "where you're working with people on a problem that's not your own." She's had to pick her spots carefully, but for the organizations she genuinely cares about and wants to succeed, she's carved out the time and space to contribute as much as she can. It's given her exposure to business leaders from other sectors who share a similar passion for causes and issues and has allowed her to tap into other networks, too.

Nonprofit boards are an incredible way to build a network. They're not low lift—I say this as a nonprofit executive who asks a medium amount of my board—but they're a unique opportunity for you to stretch your skills a bit and apply them to something outside your expertise.

Any leader good at their job will ask you for money. And caution: Many (most) nonprofit boards have some kind of fundraising requirement. Size varies, as do the mechanics of the gift (e.g., it could be a "write the check or raise that amount of money from other people" kind of mandate). This may feel frustrating or discriminatory to you—it's absolutely a barrier to entry. But from the nonprofit's perspective, it makes sense. Board members should have some financial skin in the game when it comes to the nonprofit's operating success or failure and should be helpful in supporting the organization's bottom line; some organizations have explicit rules about how much of their budget needs to come from their board. Be honest about what you can give and what kind of support you may be able to give instead of or in addition to money. Think expansively: Can you make key introductions? Find free or cheap space for something? Access a resource the organization might otherwise have trouble acquiring?

In most governing models, the board can fire or hire the executive director or, at the very least, can make the ED's job a living nightmare—so it's not always easy to wiggle your way into a seat. Approach this goal with a long time horizon for success: Pick an organization you care about, show up consistently, give what you can, and build a personal relationship with leadership. Prove you can be a value add. Yes, you're doing this for your own professional development, but if you choose wisely, the organization's mission should actually matter to you. Win-win.

If you're already in the nonprofit space, you know both how important good boards are and how hard it is to find good board members. Don't hesitate to let your colleagues who do great work know that you want to be helpful and are open to serving on their boards if a seat opens up. Just be top of mind when the moment strikes.

• • •

"Find a mentor!" is the default go-to for those giving career advice to folks more junior or rising up the ranks.

This might be easy for the guy who got the job because his dad is an executive at the company and has been chilling with the other C-suite dudes at family barbecues since he was a teenager or for people who are in professions with formalized mentorship structures. But for so many next-gen leaders, "find a mentor" feels like telling us to "catch a single snowflake and bring it home with you." It's ridiculous advice that feels divorced from reality.

For starters, next-gen leaders tend to be pushing boundaries on what a leader looks like—there often aren't as many people like us who've been in our shoes before. And unfortunately, many of those that have can often operate as if they're eager to pull up the ladder behind them.

It's not that mentors can't be from a different race, ethnicity, gender, or class background. But there are barriers, full stop. Irene Ashu, a millennial who runs her own production company specializing in experiential events, live shows, and digital and print content, described to me the challenges of being one of the few Black executives in her space. "All my mentors just happen to be white men or white women," she said, "so when talking to my mentors, the language and thought process is different.

"White mentors—not all—don't always analyze how their privilege and position of power connects to workplace dynamics," she explained. "My white-guy mentors are always like, 'Yeah, if someone doesn't like what you say, just double down on it,' and I'm like, 'That works for you, Jim—people are scared of you, in a different way.' When you're a Black woman, people have a different reaction."

She went on: "Even down to mistakes and second chances—one of my favorite mentors, he produced a really terrible festival, and he's like, 'Well, I'm just gonna make a documentary about it, and then I'm going to move on.' And I was like, that's one of the most white-guy things I've ever seen."

She doesn't hold it against them, exactly—rather, she just has to take their advice and guidance with a grain of salt. What works for them won't necessarily work for her, no matter how perfectly she implements it. It's shitty that she has to filter their advice through that lens, but it's reality.

One way she's tried to fix it moving forward: She's been proactive and intentional about mentoring junior creatives of color, knowing that she can provide insight that their other bosses might not be able to share.

This was a common theme especially among the women of color and other underrepresented next-gen leaders I spoke with: a passion for leadership development and mentorship, knowing they're filling a need for the next class of folks to make up for what they lacked earlier in their careers.

Ben Greene, a Gen Z leader and advocate for the trans community, has made community building and mentorship his entire career. He came out as trans when he was just fifteen in a town where there weren't any other openly trans people—he quickly took a leadership role running what he called an "underground organization" (meaning: an online community with no adults in it or aware of it) for LGBTQ+ young people across Connecticut.

Becoming a leader so early in his career has been isolating—his friends, understandably, just aren't at the same stage in their careers, so while they can be there for him personally, they don't always get it. "There were years where I felt like I didn't really have anybody on my side. I think I had people rooting for me, but I didn't have people on my team, and I feel like that's different," he said.

Over the years, he's gathered a small cadre of personal and professional mentors, "some of whom are in the advocacy spaces with me, some of whom are in the business space, some of whom are or aren't trans." And like so many next-gen leaders, he's taken on a more proactive mentorship role. Ben joked that his parents used to call him the "pied piper because, at any given moment, I had between five and ten terrified little baby queer kids who were kind of attached to me—they were like, 'I need you to help me figure it out. . . . I had all these [people] that I was guiding through what I had been through because nobody had been able to be that for me."

This is all beautiful—it's also a damning indictment of who's been considered a leader up until the last few years and who is *still* left out of the rooms where decisions are made. Next-gen leaders feel strongly: We may be the first, but we are adamant we won't be the last.

I come to this advice with an honest confession: Like so many of the people I talked to, I struggled with finding a mentor over the years. I was twenty-six years old (and arguably in way over my head) when we started Run for Something—there just weren't that many leaders, especially women, who'd tried to build this kind of organization before.

It took until late 2023, when Stephanie Schriock, the former president of EMILYs List, the largest organization dedicated to electing pro-choice Democratic women, took us on as a client for a related project. We ended up building a genuine relationship—we have a weekly half-hour call on the books just to check in about what's going on for me and my work. Her strategic wisdom and knowledge of the ecosystem is unmatched, as is her regular reminder to "work the problem in front of us"—a refrain meant to keep us focused on thinking through exactly what is needed to solve the current sticky situation, as opposed to spiraling out about all the possible sticky situations that could come one day down the road.

It took me over a decade in the workforce to build that relationship. Not great! So my biggest advice here is that like most things in leadership, it's not that you're bad at it—it's that finding a mentor is genuinely hard. That being said . . .

Don't ask, don't get. You can only get the help you request; it is rare someone will volunteer their time or support to you. So send the email or DM. Make it easy for them to say yes by asking for something specific: You want *X* amount of time for *A*, *B*, *C* questions, none of which can be easily answered by googling. This is a personal pet peeve of mine that you might not share, but as someone who's done a ton of interviews over the years about the origin story of my organization, getting emails asking to talk about "how I started Run for Something" makes me batty.

The best way to do this: Be clear that you are hoping for *Y* and *Z* things out of the conversation, which you will make easy for the recipient to execute on. You will follow up in a timely manner with appropriate materials as needed. Don't ask to pick someone's brain—ask them for thirty minutes of their time in order to learn more about the HR operations of their company as they scaled from ten employees to fifty to help you as you're preparing your own growing period, or whatever the details might be.

Showing someone you're not going to waste their time—and then actually not wasting it—is 80 percent of the battle. If you're seeking mentorship from someone, they're probably even busier than you are. Be thoughtful and be efficient.

Seek advice outside your company or organization. Especially if you're nearing the top of the org chart, it may be hard to find someone internally who has enough distance from your work to give you good advice. Consider reaching back out to a boss you had at a previous job or a colleague you admired but only sort of knew who no longer works directly with you. Distance helps!

Give it time. Like any and all relationships, mentorship requires a certain amount of intimacy and vulnerability. You're going to have to share your weaknesses in order to grow them into strengths (or at least neutrals). That can't happen overnight.

Instead of (or in addition to) a mentor, find a thought partner. Inspired by *Personal Math*, an online newsletter about making career decisions in your thirties, authored by boomer Greg Shove and millennial Taylor Malmsheimer: What you think you're looking for out of a mentor might also be found in a thought partner. You want someone with the context to understand what you're going through, the objectivity to force you to think differently, and the confidence in your relationship to be able to push you without fear. Not quite a therapist (definitely not a therapist!), not quite a friend (although you can be friends!), not quite a cheerleader (although they should be rooting for you! They should just be doing so without being a yes-person or a kiss-ass).

Shove and Malmsheimer suggest using language like, "I want to think out loud about this problem for a few minutes," "I want to pick your brain on something I've been grappling with," "Let's riff on this problem for a little bit," and "I'm not looking for the answer. . . . Let's just tease out the various paths."

I love this style of collaboration, but I find it's necessary to explicitly give people permission to push back on me and then celebrate them when they do. I like to use "Tell me why I'm wrong" or "What am I missing here?" in these conversations and ensure that I'm in the right headspace to hear the answers. This all requires swallowing ego and sometimes sitting on my hands. But it's worth doing.

* * *

The truth of the situation is simple: When you become a leader, especially in a work setting, you'll be responsible for other people's livelihoods. You could have the power to hire people, changing their lives (hopefully for the better) and shaping how they spend a vast portion of their waking hours. With that comes the power—and occasionally the obligation, whether for performance reasons, financial ones, or otherwise, to fire people. You'll have to have hard conversations about money, time management, prioritization, behavior, and more.

It's really, really hard to do that with people you also do karaoke with, or go out to drinks with, or spend time with one another's families. Not impossible, of course, but exponentially harder.

As you climb the ladder, you will find that your relationships change. That's not an indictment of you as a person; it's a reflection of the power dynamics.

Especially if you're not a leader yet, take the time now to build your community outside work. Find your people who you can vent to. In the context of dating, my good friend Patrick used to describe this as "be an air conditioner: cool air out the front, trash air out the back." An apt metaphor that applies to leadership, too!

• • •

If I told you an elected official had a 70 percent approval rating, you'd assume they're wildly popular (and in today's political environment, you'd be right!). But consider the flip side: Even a leader with a 70 percent approval rating has 30 percent disapproval. An extremely popular leader is still not a unanimously popular one; no leader can please everyone, no matter how hard they try.

In some ways, it's freeing to realize: No matter what you do, some people will be unhappy about it. This became clear to me back in 2022 when, as part of our organizational growth, we reset our salary ladder based on an extensive competitive analysis that would put our organization's compensation in the seventy-fifth percentile of the broader marketplace of comparably sized nonprofits. Once we set the intended new levels, we needed to bring folks' salaries up to the appropriate amounts—so after an equity analysis, we ultimately ended up giving every person at the organization at least a 30 percent raise.

You'd think people would be thrilled! More money without a commensurate increase in work or responsibility? Count me in, ten out of ten, no edits, no red flags.

Most people were! They took the pay increase, understanding it was an investment in them specifically and in our talent more broadly. But there was one report back from one of our managers that made my brain explode: One of the more junior employees who'd gotten one of the biggest raises was loudly unhappy it hadn't been more.

I fundamentally couldn't comprehend it. We had just increased this person's pay in a dramatic way that would make a meaningful difference in their life, and the company hadn't asked for anything in return. Our goal was simply to make compensation equitable and market competitive. But still, it wasn't enough.

In the years since then, as I've had to make hard decisions that may make some members of the team mad, I remind myself: I can literally throw money at people, and at least one of them is likely to complain that I threw it too hard.

I'm not saying people's feelings are useless or not worth caring about—they absolutely are, within reason. But the ways in which leadership, especially in the workplace, has expanded to include not just hitting our goals but ensuring our teammates feel good and fulfilled, find meaning, etc., along the way has changed the responsibilities of those in charge. A number of the next-gen leaders I talked to jokingly described the role as "running an adult day care."

Ziad Ahmed, Gen Z founder of a marketing agency, said point-blank that at least half his job as CEO is emotional labor. "I don't think that's what a lot of CEOs—of any generation—signed up for. They signed up to make decisions, to be strategic—but it's my job to treat concerns as legitimate, to hear people out, to make people feel seen and heard," Ziad said.

"A majority of our employees are best friends [with each other]," he explained, "so the emotional stakes of a lot of conversations are charged." He's got to act not just as a boss running a company but also occasionally as part therapist, part mediator, part listener, part coach, and even part punching bag at times.

Leadership often means making calls or saying the hard thing that not everyone will understand or agree with. While we should do our best to explain our thinking and get buy-in, even the most popular decisions will have a hater or two.

This is one of the hardest lessons new leaders and managers have to learn, especially for those of us socialized to contort ourselves to make people like us (meaning: women). You have to give hard feedback. Sometimes you will hurt people's feelings. Sometimes people will be mad at you, and they will communicate that anger in ways that then make you mad. Thus starts the vicious cycle of hurt feelings, simmering resentment, and reciprocating rage. This is not a productive place to sit in. It doesn't serve you or your mission and definitely doesn't serve your team.

So, here are a few suggestions for how to teach yourself to give less of a shit if people don't like you:

Consider a reframe: Just as having public haters means you've reached outside your echo chamber, having internal ones means you're giving people a common enemy to bond around.

Early in my career, I had a boss who would regularly leave the team happy hours after an hour or two. Later, after I stopped working for her and we could be just friends, I asked her why that was the case. She told me it was intentional. She wanted to give folks a chance to shit talk her without her there and to be free from the responsibility of being on their "best behavior." She was the common experience they all shared. It was occasionally hard on her self-esteem, but she knew it was an important space for everyone else.

I'm not saying actively create an environment of shit talking. But know that it's going to happen and there's nothing you can do about it, so it's simply easier to operate as if what others say about your leadership (especially when you're not there to hear it) is none of your business and you're doing them a public service by giving them something to bond over.

Use your integrity to build a suit of armor: If you are clear-eyed about your goals and confident about the framework you're using to make decisions, everything you do should be in service of your mission. Sometimes you have to put care for the whole above caring for the individual.

I've found that the moments the haters have gotten to me are the same moments I am my own loudest critic, when I know they're right and that I've made a decision that puts ego or feelings (mine or others') above the mission. If I piss people off and also compromise the work itself or our goals, then what was the point?

During the process of the layoffs I described earlier, I know that others were hurt, whether by losing their jobs, by feeling betrayed by the fundamental trust they had in job security, or by something else. But I know I was doing the right thing for the long-term sustainability of the organization and the ability for us to do work that mattered for as long as possible. I knew it was the right decision, even with the pain it caused, and I owned that.

Jesse Genet, millennial entrepreneur and cofounder of multiple companies, told me about a similar challenge she faced when she was deciding whether or not to sell the company she had built. "There were lots of mixed feelings from the team about my decision to do that—and I can't put that decision on anyone else. I completely owned it." She explained that she could have blamed other forces, investor opinions, market conditions, or something else entirely, but part of her leadership journey has been getting comfortable saying something that other people disagree with, as long as she knows it's right.

"The hardest thing to manage is your own psychology about your business. At the end of the day, your own opinion matters most but only if you're being really fucking honest with yourself," she explained. That's not to say that good leaders always make the right decisions: "Some people are great leaders—objectively, great leaders—even if they don't achieve great outcomes. But they believe themselves," she told me, describing the cult leader who walks people right off a cliff. Gross metaphor alert: There is a risk in drinking your own Kool-Aid so much you make yourself puke.

You need to cultivate rigorous honesty with yourself about your goals and motivations. You need to build a network of people who can and will tell you if you're doing something stupid. Take in the negative feedback—it's important to hear it. But it isn't always important to take it personally or to internalize it. Leading with integrity won't make everyone happy all the time, but that's not the goal. The goal is your mission. If you're working in service of that, you're making the right call.

• • •

David Hogg, Gen Z leader of March For Our Lives, the major gun-safety advocacy organization that came out of the 2018 shooting at a high school in Parkland, Florida, has dealt with some real bullshit. By the nature of his role as an extremely public survivor of gun violence and then advocate for gun safety, he was taking on the NRA and becoming a lightning rod for haters, all as a high school and eventually college student. He faced hostility, aggression, and even death threats that forced him to take security precautions as he worked to make guns harder to access and schools safer for kids. Especially in the early years, he was working around the clock, traveling the country to hold rallies, meet with other survivors of gun violence, and hold politicians accountable for being bought and paid for by the gun lobby.

He said he had to learn the hard way that rest was part of productivity: "There are times in the immediate aftermath of the shooting where you have to work incredibly hard, and you can't stop—you're going to get burned out, exhausted, sick, potentially even traumatized by how hard you're working, especially in the circumstances we are in—but 99 percent of the time, that's not the case," he told me. "I would work and work and work for weeks on end until I got so physically ill that I could not leave my bed."

He felt like he couldn't stop—so many "adults" (as he described them) would tell him and the other gun-violence survivors, "Thank God because you're here to save us," an unbearable amount of pressure to put on anyone, let alone a recently traumatized teenager. It took going to college, stepping back, and realizing that "if I'm not taking care of myself, I'm not doing my part to take care of the movement because I'm just one part of it."

More broadly, David described learning the lesson of "not feeling guilty about having joy, no matter how fucked up the world is." He described moments in the weeks and months after the shooting when he and the other March For Our Lives founders would do press and folks would ask for a photo with them. Naturally, they smiled. "We had memes made of us by the far right that said, 'This is the face you make when you're standing on the bodies of your dead classmates.'"

David reflected on that experience, explaining that "For all major mass shootings that get a high amount of publicity, if you're advocating on it, the right will try and tell you—basically brainwash you—into thinking that you can never be happy again because of what happened to you. Saying that to a group of fucking children is one of truly the most sinister things I've ever seen because we believed it for a long time."

He described it as the NRA attempting to steal their future capacity for joy. It took him a lot of time, growth, and healing to refind it and to build the boundaries necessary to not let the haters get to him.

You don't need to be under attack from a supremely corrupt lobbying group, or healing from a mass shooting, or facing the brute force of millions of social media followers to feel similar pressure like what David experienced: that you can't dare be happy because you have had to do or have experienced hard things.

I heard from leaders in so many conversations and have felt this myself: When we have to make tough decisions or do painful things as leaders, we sometimes feel guilty about having fun (whether at work or outside of it).

That guilt does not serve us. We are not better at our jobs if we're miserable or martyring ourselves. See a few pages earlier: Bosses have feelings, too. We can take the responsibility of our power seriously and carry the weight of our actions without self-flagellating anytime we have to do a hard thing. If you're doing the best you can and leading with integrity, don't beat yourself up too much.

• • •

We've talked through finding intentional community, building your armor of integrity, and letting go of the haters. But I'd be remiss if I didn't also bring up the need for self-care.

In Dr. Pooja Lakshmin's book, *Real Self-Care*, she explains how self-care is not just bath bombs, yoga classes, or pedicures because, as delightful as those things are, no pedicure can make up for, say, the emotional and financial stress of childcare, or the day-in, day-out grind of racism.

Self-care, Dr. Lakshmin argues, needs to be internal and threaded through your day-to-day life. You practice self-care by setting boundaries, dealing with your guilt, being compassionate toward yourself, identifying your values, and claiming your agency. That might still involve going to a yoga class but only if paired with letting go of the guilt that you went to yoga class instead of crossing something else off your to-do list.

Here are a few suggestions for how to practice self-care at work and outside it, in addition to nearly everything else we've covered in this book so far.

Think about what in your work makes you happy. You can literally keep a mood diary if that helps—write yourself a note after a meeting that sparked joy or working on a project that left you feeling energized. See if you can identify some themes.

Maybe that's through mentorship, like Mazin Sidahmed, millennial founder of *Documented* you met earlier, who gets intense satisfaction supporting folks early in their journeys. "Seeing people's careers grow, seeing people feel fulfilled in their jobs and taking more ownership" is the part he loves the most.

Similarly, Tina Cartwright, a millennial running Rebranding Motherhood, an online community trying to literally rebrand motherhood in the modern world after extensive experience in corporate America, has loved seeing the people she's mentored fly off to bigger and better things. Millennial Alida Garcia from previous chapters similarly shares a love of leadership development, especially bringing young leaders of color up through the ranks with her. She's made it into one of her side hustles, running a community that gives hiring managers access to a résumé bank from a diverse group of applicants.

For others, it's the work itself—teachers told me about the thrill of seeing their students click in new schools. Activists and politicians I spoke with talked about the impact they're able to make in people's lives; writers talked about the creative fulfillment that comes with a piece well done. I spoke with one leader in a corporate-consulting job who felt proud when they were able to facilitate a well-run meeting. I personally find deep joy in interacting with candidates and leaders and affirming for them their struggles are communal; they're not alone. (Sound familiar?)

Even a dream job is still a job. There will always be parts that suck. But as a leader, you have more power than most to focus on the things you love about it and give those as much energy as you can. Being miserable at work doesn't make your work more meaningful and rarely makes you more effective. You don't get a medal on your deathbed because you did it the hard way. If there's a part that brings you joy, lean into that. It will help take the sting out of the unavoidable parts that really hurt.

Say no so you can say yes. Sometimes finding the joy might require saying no to growth opportunities that, while challenging, would suck the fun out of the work. Sarah Kunst, a millennial in venture capital, is clear-eyed on what she wants out of her role: "People will say to me, you should run this big company," she said, "and I totally get it—but it's so not where I thrive. I would not love it, and I don't want to have to do things I don't love." She focuses her energy on building networks, especially among women of color in tech and finance, and supporting them one-on-one.

Early on in your career, you may have been the can-do kid, so to speak. You might have been the person who would take on as much as possible in order to be reliable and productive, to learn, to get a good reputation around the office—whatever the reason was, you said yes to anything asked of you. That can be a hard habit to shake! So many folks I spoke with pointed to a moment in their career where they became more discerning about which opportunities or responsibilities they took on, knowing that their time is limited and their skills are valuable.

There is an oft-repeated quote—"If it's not a hell yes, it's a no"—that's usually applied to relationships but can be similarly used in reference to career opportunities. I wouldn't go quite that far: Sometimes you should say yes to things you're meh about if they're strategic opportunities or they serve your goals in other ways.

But in service of protecting your peace, be intentional about how you spend your time. Do you *really* need to go to that happy hour, or travel to that conference, or pick up that outside-of-work effort? Check your ego—are you *really* the only person who could succeed at it? A general rule of thumb for me is "If I saw someone else taking this opportunity I was offered, would I get mad at them for doing it in a way I thought was wrong?" Sometimes the answer is yes, and so I say yes. But just as often the answer is "There are many right ways to do this, and I hope they do it one of those ways!" so I can say no without regrets.

Care for yourself. Yes, I know, I said a few paragraphs ago that self-care is more than just bath bombs and pedicures. But that doesn't mean bath bombs and pedicures (or whatever your equivalent is) aren't also great. Make time to exercise, build Magna-Tile towers with your kids, watch sports, meditate, read romance novels, play video games, pet your dog, bake brownies, or do whatever it is that helps you unwind—literally put the time on your calendar and treat it like a meeting you can't skip. Put your phone on Do Not Disturb after 10:00 p.m. and veg out to Bravo reality shows or go to bed early. You don't need to feel guilty about this.

Just as you give your team lots of vacation and leeway with their schedules—do that for yourself. Practice what you preach re being a full person out of your workplace. Yes, I'm being slightly hypocritical here, and yes, I'm calling myself out (or in, as it may be). But/and: It's really, really important. You will be a better leader when you've got a chance to breathe.

None of this functionally alters the structural challenges of leadership or the difficulties baked into living in a world with not enough safety nets and too many potholes. But you should never feel bad about trying to do things on easy mode when you can. Repeat the mantra: My suffering serves no one.

WE DO NOT DREAM OF LABOR

So far in this book, we've focused on the day-to-day lived experience of leadership—the ways we define ourselves, define our organizations and teams, and survive the hard parts. In this final section, we'll look toward the future: What comes next? What are our ambitions? How do we figure out where to climb from here when everything feels so uncertain beneath our feet?

For me, like most next-gen leaders, it's complicated.

I think often about an event I went to in fall 2023, just a few days before my oldest daughter's first birthday. It was the opening reception for a conference that kicked off by pairing us into speed-dating-type conversations with intentionally personal icebreakers.

The facilitator asked us to share: If you were 30 percent braver, what would you do to be a good ancestor?

We were told to sit silently and think about our answers for a minute before engaging with our partners. I was stuck. I consider myself pretty brave. That's not to say I'm fearless—a mouse running across our apartment floor once left me standing on the counter for a half hour—but, at least professionally, I try not to let my fear hold me back. I like to tell myself, "If you're afraid, do it afraid."

So I struggled a bit with this question about bravery. I sat mulling it over and realized that the key clause of the icebreaker question wasn't the first part but, rather, the second: What was I doing to be a good ancestor?

When the timer went off to kick us into conversation, I turned to my conversation partner, Suzette, and found myself getting personal.

"It's my daughter's first birthday this week," I said to her. "And I missed bedtime with her tonight. My husband has been texting me photos of her shoveling yogurt into her face, playing with her toys, drinking her bottle while she snuggles up with him. She'll be asleep by the time I get home later."

I went on: "I've been reflecting a lot on my first year of motherhood. I've had to travel, had to miss bedtimes, had to skip day care pickup to stay on one last call. And I really do believe that I'm doing this for her! I'm doing this to make the world a better place for my daughter and maybe for her daughter one day. But what if"—I paused, getting emotional—"what if I've chosen wrong? What if in deciding to work so hard to make a better world for her tomorrow, I'm being a worse mom for her today?

"Maybe if I was a little braver, I'd make a different choice."

Suzette leaned over to put her hand on my arm to comfort me. In an effort to be vulnerable and, ahem, brave, I shared this reflection more broadly with the room of leaders, maintaining a little more composure and with a more practiced explanation. I could see dozens of people nodding their heads.

Tiana Epps-Johnson, the democracy hero whom you met in an earlier chapter, stood up after me and reflected on the same compromise she was making: If she was working so hard to save democracy for her nephews in the future, was it worth it to have less time to spend with them now?

We joked afterward: how ridiculous it was that we sought out the bravery to work less.

I've been thinking about that question ever since, as again and again I've been faced with hard choices about what I want out of my life.

I am unabashedly ambitious. I want to make a meaningful difference in the world by doing things that interest me and challenge me. (I also have to pay the bills, and New York City with two kids is not cheap.)

At the same time, I want a joyful life with my family. I want the time and resources to be a full person with interests, hobbies, friends, and, as much as I can control it, good health. I want to work hard but not be miserable doing it.

It's not that I want to "have it all"—as we've discussed, our society as it currently exists is not set up with enough safety nets and support systems to allow me to even imagine that. But if I can't have it all, I want to have enough of the things that matter, and what "enough" looks like—and how much should be taken up by my professional life in service of that—is under constant negotiation.

As I try to answer these questions for myself, I'm conflicted. On a very macro level, I love my job. But on the micro-level, day-to-day, hour-by-hour existence, it is still a job. That means it involves work, which is by definition not all that fun and, sometimes, super unpleasant. And while the highs of work can be very high—I've been on top-leadership lists in big magazines, met presidents and celebrities, and gone on live national television—none of it has been as meaningful as, say, teaching my toddler how to do "cheers!" with her sippy cup or making the baby laugh for the first time.

These are challenges in particular for women and especially new parents but not exclusively for either community. I heard similar sentiments from people across the gender spectrum, earlier than the typical midlife crisis age you'd expect, and from parents and nonparents alike. Nearly every leader I spoke with was questioning whether the hustle was worth the sacrifices it required.

And yet: We *are* ambitious! We are strivers. That ambition is how we rose through the ranks and took on big leadership roles. But for so many of us, that description is missing a second part. We are ambitious for ________—for rest, or balance, or joy, or financial security, or meaning. We want more than just a title. Many of us have realized: While money and financial security are must-haves, there is a limit to how much joy a full bank account can bring us. (Mandatory privilege check here: This is only something someone can seek because they have a certain amount of confidence that their basic needs are being met.)

As next-gen leaders in particular, our ambitions are constantly changing as the ground beneath us shifts rapidly. The career paths available to our former bosses and our parents no longer exist for us, and new ones seem to spring up overnight that we can take advantage of if we want to.

Others still are struggling with what it means to peak early in your career and look ahead to another few decades in the workforce that feels like they could be a long downward slide.

So in this final chapter, we'll consider what it means to be ambitious for more than just a job and answer the question: Why do next-gen leaders feel this way?

Then, because even as we want to live full lives outside of work, we still need (and want!) to work—so we'll get into the changing nature of career paths. It's no longer the norm to be working at the same major corporation for twenty years where you climb the ladder slowly but methodically. Knowing that, how do you decide what to do next?

After that, an examination of one of the maxims of next-gen leadership—that the way things were are not the way things have to be—as it relates to our career trajectories. As next-gen leaders are shaping our own career paths with a different vision of what a good life looks like we're literally reshaping how we run our companies and our lives.

• • •

The title of this chapter comes from a tweet (sorry) of a quote that some people on the internet seem to think was attributed to James Baldwin, although I can't find verified proof, so make of that what you will. The sentiment was simple:

I don't have a dream job because I do not dream of labor.

I love this sentiment. A "dream job" implies that there is an occupation or place of employment that can satisfy everything you want out of life, and as we discussed earlier, work simply cannot be the space for everything. That's not to say there can't be good jobs, or jobs that are better suited to your skills, or jobs you even enjoy doing, but any job that is called "a dream" will inherently fail to live up to those expectations.

And don't forget: A nightmare is a kind of dream, too.

Rainesford Stauffer literally wrote the book on this in 2023 when she published *All the Gold Stars*, a deep dive into the changing nature of ambition for millennials and Gen Z. She argued that institutions have failed us and career ladders that were supposed to exist crumbled. Ambition and personal achievement were framed as an individual solution to what were actually major structural problems.

"For a lot of the people I spoke to," Rainesford said to me, "they'd get the promotion or start the business—they did do this thing that mattered to them, and then it eventually felt a little bit empty." Their relationship to work and to accomplishments began to shift.

"This idea that I've sacrificed my body, my physical health, my mental health, my sense of self, my time, my friendships, my relationships, and I've gotten this thing I always wanted," she explained, recounting the many interviews she did where her subjects would find themselves asking what all that sacrifice was for.

Having a goal is good! It's when achieving that goal becomes the entirety of your identity that you're in trouble, Rainesford argued. Much like your finances, your diet, and everything else, the components that make up your self-actualization need to be diversified.

For so many millennials and Gen Zers, professional goals have made up much of that list up until now. We were told all through our childhoods and adolescences that "if you love what you do you'll never work a day in your life" and if we simply followed our passions, we'd find our callings. At the same time, so many of us were pushed to work harder, achieve more, climb the ranks, get the best grades—millennials especially were raised to be "optimized," from school straight through to the workplace.[1]

That was all a well-intended load of bullshit that set us up to fail or, at least, set us up for disappointment. Next-gen leaders have felt that firsthand and are figuring out a new way forward with a more calibrated idea of what achievement and accomplishment means and a more expansive definition of what a good life looks like. It's noteworthy that per a 2025 survey, only 6 percent of Gen Z workers say their primary goal is to reach a leadership position. Instead, they're focused on work-life balance.[1]

Congresswoman Lauren Underwood, a millennial representing a suburban Chicago district in the US House of Representatives, described the tension to me: "I love the idea of setting ambitious goals, achieving them, and making a difference. This experience has taught me there's nothing I can't do. The question is: Do I actually want it? Because I know I can do it." She has self-confidence—well-earned from winning multiple hard elections against the odds and over the doubts of naysayers—to know that she is capable of anything she sets her mind to.

"It's really tough to distinguish between opportunity and affirming that's what you want," she said, explaining that discerning between what is expected of her and what she actually wants to achieve is the challenge. "I try to honor why I got into this in the first place and check myself routinely."

I asked about her vision for her future: "I want to retire early. I want to be able to send my grandkids twenty dollars for every holiday. I want to be able to go out on a Tuesday, just get dressed for no reason, go to lunch with my girlfriends, and spend all afternoon giggling because we're just living our best lives."

Lauren, from her perch in the highest echelons of the federal government, absolutely understands what next-gen leaders have dealt with: "Financial security is something we've seen in others," she said, but at the same time, she noted, we've also seen how hard it is to hold on to. "People assume that we [leaders] are disconnected from that experience. I graduated from college in 2008. I just happen to have gone to graduate school [for nursing] instead of being in the job market [during the beginning of the Great Recession]."

That economic insecurity is baked into next-gen leaders' ambitions, especially for millennials. But as Lauren clarified, "I used to be like, 'Oh, I want to be rich.' But what does that even mean? Now I'm saying I just want to have a quiet life and know that I did some good. I want to be able to walk away from all this confident that what we did mattered and made a difference."

Consider how many times over the years millennials and Gen Zers have seen hard work, big bets, and major job titles fail to bring happiness, satisfaction, or even long-term financial stability. While we are not unusual in living through unprecedented times, it does feel particularly acute for us. Whether it was entering the workforce during the recession in 2008 or trying to climb the ranks during the early days of COVID in 2020, so many of us have been forced time and again to ask: What's the fucking point? We've seen or experienced the bottom falling out beneath us all the damn time.

Everything we've talked about in this book so far—responsibly authentic leadership personas, creating spaces to be your real self but not your full self, work-life integration, all of it—is both in service of our goals but also an effort to adapt to our generation's changing relationship to ambition. If you're putting all of that into practice, you are setting yourself (and your team!) up to be more than just a professional identity or job title.

If your leadership persona includes building connections over books or sports teams or cupcake recipes, you can be more than just the robot boss. If your team norms are such that civic engagement is encouraged and enabled, then you have the space to be a good citizen. If you have a workplace that encourages and enables you to take family leave and block out time for school drop-off, you can actually be a present parent as well as an effective leader.

We do all of this because it gets the job done. We also do all of this because it frees us to be more than just our jobs.

• • •

Even if we do not dream of labor, nearly all of us still have to work for a living. We've got bills to pay, mouths to feed, dogs to keep comfortable, student loans to pay off, all of that and more.

The framework through which we decide what to do in our careers has changed a lot over the last few decades and is especially challenging once we've risen up the leadership ladder. While it has always been typical for twentysomethings to job hop as they figure their shit out, Gallup research has shown that millennials are *currently* the most likely generation to switch jobs—college graduates could have a dozen jobs by their thirties—and it's fair to assume the research will show similar stats about Gen Z, if not even more dramatic numbers, once they've been in the workforce long enough.

What's different for us is that in past generations, people would (generally speaking) become bosses after a few decades at the same company. They'd climb the ladder slowly and methodically over time, then once they got to the top, they'd stay there, come hell or high water. Combined with a broader delay in retiring and people living longer lives than generations before us, boomers have stayed in charge, preventing upward mobility for everyone else. (Sorry to Gen X.)

But we're at a breaking point. As generational turnover in leadership starts to happen across nearly every sector, we're going to see next-gen leaders take power earlier in their lives than the generations before us. We're climbing faster and going higher, and we're going to have to do it all for even longer. It's no longer the norm to stay at a job or a leadership role for twenty-plus years—so how do we pick what to do next? How do we know where to go when the future feels so uncertain? How do we create a straight line out of a bunch of crooked leaps?

KP Trueblood, millennial president of the Brooklyn Museum whom you met briefly earlier, described it simply: "Careers are galaxies." While for some industries it's a clear path, for most of us, we are bouncing around toward an ultimate North Star.

Take her, for example: KP grew up moving around the country a bit but ultimately landed at the University of Washington in Seattle, where she joined the Air National Guard, part of the United States Air Force, to help pay for college. She got a master's in public policy from the Paris Institute of Political Studies and did a stint working for NGOs in India and Cambodia. Upon graduation, she went to DC to work for a US senator doing district outreach work, then moved over to the Department of the Treasury, working up through the budget and management offices to gather more experience with federal government administrative work. That led her to a job running White House operations for President Obama in 2013, and then moving over to the Hillary Clinton campaign (where we met!) as she served as the deputy chief financial officer and the budget director.

She was chief operating officer of the Clinton transition team (whomp whomp), then when that fell through, joined the ACLU as chief of staff. After nearly five very long and hard years in advocacy work, KP landed at the Brooklyn Museum, overseeing essentially everything that isn't actually art—the budget, operations, the building, the staff, and more. Her job ties together her long-standing passion for art, culture, and institutions that are trying to change the world.

KP says, "I tell my story like it was this beautifully orchestrated thing—but for every phenomenal job offer I've gotten, I have hundreds of rejections in the file." She hasn't let that discourage her. In fact, those moments of failure have given her the intel she needed to progress: "I always ask for feedback when I don't get a job offer—sometimes it's a little bit bullshit, but a lot of times they will tell you the thing that the other candidate edged you out on. And so then I think going in, 'I need to figure out how to do that next.'"

Like so many of the leaders I spoke to, KP is ambitious but not in the way she might have defined it earlier in her career, when it was "a title and organization. That's evolved now to:

I'm just really interested in working on hard problems with mission-driven organizations that align with what I believe about the world."

Millennial Sali Christeson, founder of women's work-wear brand Argent, embodies that kind of jumping-around mentality perfectly. After a few years working in consulting and then a decade at Cisco, a global tech company, Sali founded Argent. She had no background in fashion or apparel, but she identified a problem—women's work wear mostly sucked—and had a vision for how to solve it.

She found a creative partner, built the branding out, and strategically launched it by showing up at conferences with thousands of women in attendance in order to put the product in front of them. Sali explained her seemingly chaotic choice as deeply intentional: "I had read that a nonlinear career path keeps you innovative—bouncing around is really good for you."

She self-identifies as an entrepreneur at heart and knew she'd eventually found her own company at some point, so she chose a corporate path that would allow her to understand all the functions of business. Sali's job at Cisco involved a leadership rotational program that helped her really understand communication—"My favorite quote is 'If I had more time, I would have written a shorter email,'" she said—and then took on a role that had her ultimately leading a team that grew from seven to 250. It was incredibly hard and pushed her but also helped her find the confidence needed to ultimately step out on her own and build something herself. Eight years in, Argent is a successful and well-known brand that celebrities, politicians, and totally normal people (like me!) wear and, thanks to Sali's intentionality about values-infused work, also a driver of community among high-powered women. The company (and Sali) regularly hosts events, bringing together leaders across different sectors to learn and grow together.

Sali said point-blank: "This path doesn't make sense for me at all, right? I was on a fast track in tech. But that didn't fill my cup in the same way this does, and I really have to be in a job that does that."

I heard similar echoes of joy and ambition in my conversation with Masako Morishita, a millennial chef in DC. She got her start as an executive assistant and later spent five years as a professional cheerleader for the Washington Commanders, including one year as team captain. Being a cheerleader was part-time, so she'd go to her day job as an office manager at a Japanese media company, then go to practice after work a few times a week, along with workouts on her own, and then show up every game day six hours before the game started.

The time on the Commanders taught her how to work hard, put in the effort, and deal with pressure under the spotlight. "Dancing and kitchens—they're completely different things!" Masako said, smiling. "But I'm doing the exact same thing I did at the Commanders. I look at each of my teammates and let them know: I see you."

Now as a star in the food world—she won a major James Beard Award in 2024—she's embracing that pressure as she leads her team through it, working as hard as they do, and finding the love and joy in cooking and creating new dishes.

She admits, "I have no backups, nobody who can support me. I think maybe a lot of immigrant women are like me—they have their goals and dreams, but they can't really step forward because they're scared, just like I was." She hopes her path and success can inspire them or, at the very least, show that where you start does not need to define where you end.

• • •

The concept of "passion work" comes up a lot for next-gen leaders, who generally have looked to take on jobs that align with their values and give them meaning.

This makes sense, according to Dr. Erin A. Cech, an associate professor at University of Michigan and author of *The Trouble with Passion: How Searching for Fulfillment at Work Fosters Inequality*.

She makes the case that who we are and what we do are fundamentally intertwined—it's telling that when we ask kids, "What do you want to be when you grow up?" we expect them to answer with a profession, not a personal quality or community goal. Her research shows that more than 70 percent of college-educated workers in America praise "passion-related considerations" as part of their career decision-making, and almost two-thirds rank it higher than things like good salaries; this is true across gender, race, and class divides.

Passion for your work isn't just about a good job; it's about having a good life.

Millennials and Gen Zers are obviously not alone in taking on passion work—but unlike our parents and grandparents, many of us were told throughout our childhoods and adolescences to "find our passion!!" and "If you do what you love, you'll never work a day in your life!!" Centering our passion (and our sense of self) in our employment was framed as a positive moral choice.

Alas, we've learned the hard way that while that sounds good in theory, in practice, it can drain you. When we spoke, millennial Dr. Kyle Bukowski was working as chief medical officer at Planned Parenthood of Maryland but was preparing to leave for a role in the health-care industry that was less political.

He told me, "It's hard to spend all day at work, where work is completely political, and then find the energy to engage in other political activities or even just look at the world. I care so deeply about abortion access, abortion rights, and reproductive rights, and it would be nice to have some of that energy for going to a rally, or posting on social media, or having a conversation with somebody—but because this is work, I don't really want to talk about it anymore" once he leaves the office. "My political and professional roles have been matched for ten years," he said—after all that time, he was ready for separation.

I felt this in my bones. Politics is my job—and in many, many ways, I love that! But as politics generally has sucked up more of the monoculture and gotten even more depressing, I find that after ten hours of thinking about politics for work, I want to turn my brain off. While I'm a news junkie as an occupational hazard, I find when I need to decompress, I go to romance novels or podcasts about things I have absolutely no opinion about. I can't get mad about the hosts' opinions about the movie if I've never seen it—I can just listen for vibes.

If your leadership is of the passion-driven variety—whether at work or outside of it—you may be familiar with the sense that the thing you love is actively being ruined by working on it. I talked with leaders in publishing who got into it because they loved books and then found being inside the bookmaking machine made it hard for them to read for fun, leaders in Hollywood who couldn't watch a movie without seeing all the machinery behind it.

I came back often to my conversation with Marshall Hatch Jr., a millennial ordained minister and nonprofit founder in Chicago. Marshall works in the same church as his dad, the senior pastor, and the pressure on him to ultimately assume the same position in the community one day is unyielding, from all sides.

But Marshall has surprised himself as he turned away from the familial expectations, instead growing his work outside the pulpit. In 2017, he cofounded the MAAFA Redemption Project, a faith-based residential institute for young people impacted by gun violence to heal and grow.

In the process, he's imagining a different path for himself. "I'm definitely ambitious because I sincerely believe I'm here for a reason—ambition, to me, is tied into self-confidence and self-concept," he affirmed, but the idea of a single career path one is called to, like faith leadership, feels less true to him. "There are multiple callings, multiple inflections, multiple spaces within [a vocational calling] that will fit you—I'm open to those possibilities."

Marshall, a married father of two, finds himself struggling with the tension between how much he can give to his job and how much he'd have left of himself to give to his family. Next-gen leaders of all industries feel that, as the jobs we ostensibly love require more and more of our time, energy, and emotional regulation.

This is a particularly newish challenge for next-generation men, as the expectations for dads have changed and increased. In 1982, 43 percent of fathers admitted, I hope with some embarrassment, that they'd never changed a diaper; that number plummeted by 2018 down to 3 percent. With the definition of "good fatherhood" changing, working dads (a new hot term, get it trending!) are starting to experience what working moms have felt for decades: the untenable realities of trying to be on top of their game at home and at work.

The reality is, we're all struggling. Even if our job is our heart's work, our passion with a paycheck, our fullest and wildest imagination come to life—the work we do for money cannot and will not love us back. We cannot let our work slurp us up whole because, eventually, it will spit us back out.

As you consider your own career path, here are a few questions to ruminate on.

What do you want your relationship to paid work to be? How much do you want your identity wrapped up in your career? If the answer is "fully" or "mostly," what does that mean for how you literally spend your time? (And if that really is your answer, I gently but lovingly suggest revisiting that with a mental health professional.)

What does the ideal day look like for you, especially if it's a day spent working? Are you in meetings all day, or behind a computer, or a mix of both? Do you travel? Do you have to or want to live a public life? What are the lived-in details you're seeking? As Annie Dillard put it: The way we spend our days is the way we spend our lives. Do you want to spend your life sending emails? There's nothing wrong with that, but you should choose it, not fall into it.

What do you actually need? I mean that in every sense of the word: Do you need money? How much? Health care? Meaning? Dignity? Joy? There are no wrong answers here, only the answers that are wrong for you. I think about career decisions the way I think about New York City apartments: You can't get in-unit laundry *and* a third bedroom *and* outdoor space *and* interesting structural details *and* a reasonable rent price all in one—what are you willing to compromise on?

What do you like, and what do you hate? Look back on the various jobs and roles you've had over the years and consider them as broken-down parts. Did you mostly hate your job as a social media consultant, except for the creative brainstorming? Did you love your job in retail because of how much you got to interact with strangers in small doses all day? Treat your career trajectory so far like a piece of art and critique it accordingly:

What did it make you feel and why? There are no right or wrong answers, simply useful ones that help you understand what you're actually seeking.

What do you want to learn? A real challenge I've faced as a leader and that I heard come up in many of my conversations with next-gen leaders is that once you're in charge, it can be hard to make intentional time for professional or personal development. We have to do it. Professional development doesn't have to be seminars or workshops (although both of those are great options)—you can read books like this one, get into a volunteer effort that challenges in you a new way, or take on a hobby that stretches your brain in a different direction. It all counts.

What could your galaxy look like? Where you're at now does not determine where you might be in two years, five years, or twenty years. Unlike in generations past, changing jobs or even entire career paths is relatively normal. As you wrap your head around what you want your day-to-day to look like, think expansively about your journey so far and what the next chapter could be.

• • •

One overarching rule for next-gen leadership is a simple, freeing statement: The way things were done yesterday is not the way they have to be done tomorrow. As next-gen leaders, we get a chance to reshape the world—both broadly and specifically in our spheres of influence.

I noticed this particularly in the way leaders have paved career paths that reflect their values and give them the space to live the kinds of full lives they want without sacrificing success. Cooking and motherhood creator/cookbook author/Substack writer/podcaster millennial Caroline Chambers's leadership shows up in the community she's cultivating one Instagram DM at a time.

A lot of the leaders I talked to self-identify as type A, detail oriented, hyperfocused—not Caroline. She claims her type B, loosey-goosey vibes with everything she's got. After years working behind the scenes as a recipe developer for cooking magazines and cookbooks, she started sharing more of her life on Instagram as a way to kill time in the bleak days of 2020.

She bounced between content about her own postpartum experiences and recipes she could quickly and easily cook for her towheaded toddlers (without sacrificing taste and sophistication for grown-ups) and slowly built up an audience eager to find new things to cook during the early days of the pandemic. When she started *What To Cook When You Don't Feel Like Cooking*, a newsletter to put those recipes into people's inboxes, she found people would actually pay for the content and slowly built her paying audience to ultimately become the top food newsletter on the platform at the time we spoke, with nearly twenty thousand paid subscribers just a few years in.

Between that, paid sponsorships on her Instagram, ads on her podcast, and cookbook deals and sales that skyrocket to the top of the bestseller lists almost immediately because of the community she's cultivated, she told me she's doing just fine.

I asked Caroline who she models her career off of—she paused for a moment, unsure if she had an answer, then told me: "Melissa Clark [has been] a columnist for *The New York Times* cooking section for approximately a thousand years, and she's written cookbooks based on that column—she's very well-known for just this one thing. People will ask me about the future of *What To Cook When You Don't Feel Like Cooking*, and I'm like, 'I hope you have it forever.' . . . It's my Melissa Clark column." She wants her work to grow with her through the stages of life, while acknowledging that she's not quite a food blogger, "which has been the traditional path for women in the food space."

In the new iteration of the subscription economy, Caroline is one of the leading voices, rejecting formal institutions in favor of her own platforms. She's been in conversations about hosting a cooking show but has been sadly surprised to learn that for the hours required, the pay does not come close to matching what she can make on her own and likely doesn't have the same kind of viewership either.

Caroline's thrilled to have the success she does, but she'll fully admit: It's exhausting to live life on the internet. She has to be supercareful which words she uses and adds caveats to her own choices, especially around how she parents her three sons. Caroline is also transparent about the support system she's had to build around herself to enable this career. She has paid help with tasks like cleaning, childcare, editing, schedule management, and more, which she owns as a privilege, and she described the choice to outsource what she can as a way to help her live the fullest possible life, which for her means prioritizing time with her kids.

Caroline's career path (which I would summarize as "influencer plus") is one that some research shows upward of 57 percent of Gen Z in particular aspires to take on for themselves—arguably demonstrating that the true dividing line between generations is "thinks being an influencer is unimaginable or even embarrassing" and "thinks being an influencer is a realistic way to make a living."

DeAndre Brown, a Gen Z influencer and consultant, didn't share that aspiration at first—fresh out of college, he got a job at Citibank as an analyst, working around the clock. He blew off steam by making TikToks about his experience as a young Black man in a classic corporate environment, writing and performing sketches imitating job interviews and conversations with bosses and encouraging his followers to be "corporate baddies."

His audience grew and grew, and with it, his sponsorship opportunities expanded. Ultimately after less than a year in corporate America, his career as an influencer took off, and he left Citibank to focus on his platform as well as launch GenXL Consulting, which does a mix of supporting other influencers and corporate consulting to advise companies on how to retain Gen Z employees.

DeAndre's social media presence is both his primary income stream as well as the source for his business development—a common story for so many new leaders. This creates some additional challenges. DeAndre was just starting to build out his consulting team when we spoke and was grappling with the tension that so many new bosses have to come to terms with: how to be demanding for results while staying human and compassionate. "I understand a little more why it was difficult for these people to have strong boundaries," he said, reflecting on his time in corporate environments.

Influencer as a career path is harder than it looks, and is more than just nonstop posting. "It has been very difficult to maintain that work-life balance that I preach about online, simply because a part of work is my life. I've been really working on finding that again," DeAndre explained. "Being an influencer has made [relationships with people] difficult because you're like, 'Oh you're recording,' or you don't know who's using you and who's genuine." Before he made it his career, social media was fun—it was a hobby. "So now when your hobby becomes work, it's like, now how do I find new hobbies?"

He's figuring it out one day at a time as he builds his own operation himself, outside the confines of corporate America while still somewhat reliant on corporate America, a difficult tension to grapple with.

You don't have to be an influencer or Extremely Online to shape your own career path. I talked with many next-gen leaders who struck out on their own across various industries—media, marketing, freelance strategy work, technology, and more—and so many of them echoed a similar sentiment: If I'm going to fail, I'm going to do it on my terms.

I know this from experience. When Run for Something was just an idea and some brainstorming notes in a Google Doc, I saw a social media post from a former boss who'd worked in politics for decades who said something along the lines of: If you're waiting for the adults in the room to tell you what to do now, post–2016 election, stop waiting. There are no adults. You are the adult. You see a problem? Solve it.

That stuck with me. When Ross and I started Run for Something, almost no one outside of friends and family was following me on social media, I had no experience talking to the press, and we had no start-up capital beyond what I could afford to put on my credit card to cover the Squarespace fees. I'd taken on a contract job helping a candidate launch their gubernatorial campaign to pay the bills for two months, and the advance I got for my first book helped cover my necessities until we'd raised enough money to start to pay ourselves somewhat meager salaries a few months later.

From the jump, Ross and I knew we wanted to build the organization differently. We wanted to try to lead differently, manage differently, focus in a different way—we wanted to try to combat the broken system of how things had been done on the left.

We didn't succeed in every way, of course. We have fallen prey to the boom-and-bust funding cycles, we've had to make hard choices, and we've failed and fucked up over the years. But I am proud that we've built an organization that resists the broader industry's culture of misery in service of one's mission. We've left behind the institutions who professionally raised us and laid the groundwork to build one of our own.

Not everyone is meant to be an entrepreneur, or a freelancer with minimal stability, or a serial start-up builder. It's a wild ride. But harkening back to that initial icebreaker from earlier, ask yourself: What would I do if I was just 30 percent braver?

CONCLUSION

All the way back in the introduction, I spoke specifically to a few groups of people, so that no matter who you are, you were in the right mindset to read this book. To borrow some corporate jargon: Let's close the loop.

If you're a boomer or Gen Xer: First, sorry if I offended you. (In my defense, I warned you!) The good news for you is that while next-gen leadership is certainly shaped by the years and times we grew up in, it is just as much defined by a state of mind and a set of behaviors. Regardless of your age or generation, you *can* break old habits. In fact, I'd argue that you *need* to break old habits in order to succeed because, in all likelihood, your teams are going to be demanding all the things we've talked through.

We'll all be better off if you're able to adapt. You have full permission and encouragement to try new things, adjust your policies, and show up as your responsibly authentic self. Take what might work for you—the scary-but-exciting freedom next-gen leaders have is available to you, too.

If you're not yet a leader: You might be thinking: Why the fuck would I ever want to take on more responsibility or seek that promotion? Everything I've read in this book makes it seem horrible.

It can be! But let me tell you, when it works, there is nothing better. When your team is firing on all cylinders, when you hit your goals, when you realize that the four-day workweek you fought so hard to set up is in place and you have time on Friday mornings to get in that longer run or go on a breakfast date with your partner or just flop on the couch and then go into your weekend actually rested and ready to be fun again—it is so, so, so worth it.

Taking charge is scary, but fear is an emotion, not an excuse. When your moment comes, you can do this.

Consider the alternative, too: If you don't take on the big, sticky leadership roles, someone else will, and they might not come to it with the same eagerness for work-rest integration or the deep urgency to create equitable workplaces. If you're the kind of person who thinks intentionally about any of this stuff, you're the kind of person we want and need in positions of power.

If your leadership is outside of work: I hope at least some of this was helpful! May your volunteer group meetings be well run and your social media presence be in service of your goals.

If you're already a leader: You're doing it! You can keep doing it! You deserve to be doing it!

I know it can often feel like you're just not up to the task at hand. But when you take on a leadership position, it is rarely by accident. Sure, there are many examples of people failing up. But usually, if you're in charge, it's because you're ready to be. Whether you took the initiative to build your own power or someone hired you or chose you to lead, you have proved simply by reaching that point that you *can* handle it.

When you show up determined to make only new mistakes—not repeat the old ones—you're doing the damn thing, and that *really* matters.

When workplaces are more equitable, life is better. When more people can live full lives and have the resources and time to be more than just worker bees, everyone is happier.

When leaders can hold firm boundaries that allow everyone to show up honestly but intentionally and when teams clearly understand what is expected of them and what will not be tolerated—when we can do all that while hitting our goals and delivering on our missions, everyone thrives.

As I had hundreds of formal and informal conversations for this book, the thing I kept hearing echoed across people of different sectors, industries, races, classes, genders, and specialties is how we all feel like we're never quite doing it right.

I reject the premise that there is a singular "right" way to do it anymore. What I've lived and learned about next-gen leadership is simply (and ironically) that it's complicated.

We want to be authentic and be ourselves—but we can't be fully ourselves without overburdening our teams or opening ourselves up to those who haven't earned or can't be trusted with our vulnerability. We are actively wrestling with what it means to be authentic in the AI era.

We want to be professional—but what "professional" means is rapidly changing (and we're both spurring that change and trying to ride the wave).

We have been online our whole lives, but now that we're in positions of power, we have to be more careful about how we engage, fighting years of habits.

We believe work should be a place where you *can* be your real self, but you don't have to be your full self—and that work-rest integration is absolutely possible but also hard to do and harder still to model. We want four-day workweeks, paid family leave, and generous vacation policies, and we want to do it in a way that still allows us to hit our goals. We want to be good bosses who get things done while also being good people who treat others well.

We want to build equitable and inclusive work environments but understand that to do so means being exclusive about keeping assholes out.

We want to be transparent, open, and honest, but we're learning the hard way that sometimes a little bit of opacity is a good thing, too.

We are lonely—so very lonely—and are butting up against practical realities that make it hard to build community. (We're trying, though.) We want to do more than survive our leadership roles; we want to thrive in them, but we know that taking a stand inevitably brings out the haters.

We don't have dream jobs but, rather, dream lives. We want to be more than just our professional identities—but also, we have to work for a living, and we're likely going to have to for much longer than those who came before us, so we are figuring it all out as we go.

The leadership model that made sense for the mostly older, white, male leaders of the past doesn't work for us, and it definitely doesn't work for our teams, who in the years to come will be predominantly millennials and Gen Zers who share our demands for humanity and compassion in the workplace.

Instead, we have infinite leadership models. The number of playbooks has grown exponentially as we've brought our diverse values and our just-as-diverse backgrounds with us into positions of power. We get to be the bosses we wish we'd had earlier in our careers.

We're redefining leadership as we go, both at work and outside of it. In the coming years, new politicians will be taking office, new CEOs will take the reins, new celebrities and influencers will come into the spotlight—and they (you! we!) will expand our collective imagination about what could be. In the process, we'll reshape the economy, communities, and our relationships to work, to rest, and to purpose.

When *we're* in charge, just about *anything* and maybe even *everything* is possible.

ACKNOWLEDGMENTS

In the spirit of transparency: 2024 was mostly bullshit. After the layoffs you read about and related organizational challenges, I worked as hard as I could to raise the money we needed, held on tight through an emotional roller coaster of an election that took me from resigned to hopeful to devastated, and then unfortunately had to restructure the organization again to ensure long-term sustainability.

Plus, I had a one-year-old and was pregnant with my second kid. (Nothing like a hard deadline of childbirth to make you finish a draft!)

Writing this book and getting through the year with my sanity mostly intact was only possible because of the incredible community around me.

When We're in Charge began as a germ of an idea during my year as a 2022–2023 Dial Fellow at Emerson Collective—a fellowship I began just weeks before giving birth to my first daughter. When I came back to work in the spring, still deep in the postpartum fog, the fellowship team pushed me to refind my voice and come up with something new to say.

I would not have found the time to start writing if not for the accountability I had to the fellowship, so thank you to the Emerson team—especially Ben Wessel, Megan Dino, Patrick D'Arcy, Marcy Stech, and my communications coach, Jess McIntosh, who gave me invaluable feedback and kept prodding me to think bigger.

I am unendingly grateful to my agent, Stephanie Delman, for taking that idea, helping me shape it into a proposal, and then finding it a good home at Zando. Stephanie, you've changed my life for the better at least twice now—I'm so glad you slid into my DMs all those years ago! Thanks to your entire team at Trellis, especially Elizabeth Pratt, who have shown incredible patience at my stupid questions.

Thanks to my editor, Sarah Ried, for your thoughtful edits and guidance as we took the mess of a brain-dump from my experience and interviews and turned it into something (hopefully) readable and useful. You fully understood from day one what I wanted to say and have been an unbelievable partner in helping me say it.

Thank you to everyone at Zando Projects, especially Sam Mitchell, Nathalie Ramirez, Anna Hall, Shayna Holmes, Kayla White, Andrew Rein, Ashley Alberico, and Molly Stern. And thank you to my fantastic publishing partners Jon Lovett, Jon Favreau, Tommy Vietor, Lucinda Treat, and all the other folks at Crooked Media Reads. Plus thanks to the entire Crooked Media team, especially Shaniqua McClendon, who've been great partners over the years.

To everyone who spoke to me about their leadership styles for this book—thanks for taking time out of your one precious life to tell me about what you were experiencing, how you were feeling, and what it meant to you to be in charge in a different way:

Amanda Herring Selz, Anne Helen Petersen, Adam Barney, Adele McClure, Alida Garcia, Alli King, Allison Byers, Anderson Clayton, Ann Friedman, Anna Eskamani, Annie Wu Henry, Aria Flood, Arteen Arabshahi, Ashley Lynn Priore, Ashley Spivey, Ben Greene, Cadence Hardenbergh, Caitlin Tew, Caroline Chambers, Carrie Melissa Jones, Chris Petros, Dan Egol, Danielle Curtis, Danielle Deiseroth, Danielle Moore, David Hogg, David Meadvin, DeAndre Brown, Dom Kelly, Drew Miller, Elise Joshi, Elizabeth Jackson-Rietz, Emily Reilly, Erica Mosca, Evan Spiegel, Eve Samborn, Georgie-Ann Getton, Gillea Allison, Heidi Schmidt, Ilana Glazer, Irene Ashu, Jace Woodrum, Jared Dewey, Jason Kander, Jasper Wang, Jean Theron Willoughby, Jenn Stowe, Jeremy Smith, Jesse Genet, Jessica Barolsky, Jessica Post, Jill Felska, Jonah Perlin, Jordan Harrod, Karl Catarata, Kate Catherall, Kate Watson Moss, Katie Weiss, Kayla Young, Kendra Lewis, Kevin Alster, Kodi Crow, Krissy Wall, Kyle Bukowski, Lauren Spranger, Lauren Underwood, Layla Zaidane, Libby Leffler, Lindsay Jean Thomson, Lisa Conn, Louise Yeung, Macy Stockton, Malinda Frevert, Marci Robles, Mari Manoogian, Maria Tchijov, Marshall Hatch Jr., Masako Morishita, Matt Edelstein, Maurice Mitchell, Max Lubin, Maxwell Frost, Mazin Sidahmed, Megan Sip, Michelle Finocchi, Mike Marotti, Nat Welch, Nadya Okamoto, Ndubuisi Uchea, Nikki Stokes-Thompson, Paige Port Orell, Rachel Janfaza, Rachel Lobdell, Raena Boston, Rainesford Stauffer, Rhena Hicks, Rigel Robinson, Ruwa Romman, Sabrina Hersi Issa, Sali Christeson, Sami Sage, Sara Jacobs, Sarah Kunst, Sarah Montana, Sasha Stewart, Scott Warren, Seema Thakkar, Sera Capriotti, Sergio Plaza, Sophia Zaia, Stephanie Cheng, Stephanie Llanes, Tiana Epps-Johnson, Tiara Mack, Tina Cartwright, Tom Schroeder, Tori Dunlap, Travis Hammill, Vanessa Mbonu, Veronica Tessler, Versha Sharma, Vinuri Ranaweera, Zach Wahls, Zachary Mallory, Zachary Richner, and Ziad Ahmed.

Whether our conversations are quoted in the book or not, you directly shaped my understanding of next-gen leadership and taught me so much about what it means to be in charge. I am also grateful to the many others who spoke to me off the record or in casual conversation about this work over the years, and to the hundreds of Run for Something candidates and alum I've gotten to know personally who have shown what new leadership can look like in government.

To everyone who's been part of the Run for Something team since 2017—thank you for trusting me, for your patience and gentle (or, ahem, not so gentle) feedback as I learned how to lead in real time, and most importantly, for your hard work toward our critical mission.

A special thanks to my cofounder and partner in not-crime for most of the last decade, Ross Morales Rocketto. I'm so grateful to have never been fully alone in this over the years—your strategic vision and empathy made me a better leader and person. There is no one I'd rather have gone through the bad days (and the really good days!) with.

Similarly, thanks in particular to the RFS executive team of 2023–2024—Cassandra Gaddo, Sara Hadad, Ciara Walton, Marisa Feehan, Jordan Haines, Abe Rakov, and Johanna Silva Waki—for bringing your wisdom and experience to the organization and for holding us accountable to live our values, even when it sucked.

To Kayley Rodriguez, my incredible assistant, thank you for staying on top of my inbox and schedule, for your efficiency in keeping all the balls in the air, and for bringing a patient and joyful attitude to our work together.

More broadly, I'm grateful to everyone who has made Run for Something possible, including our candidates, donors, partners, volunteers, consultants, board members, and supporters of all kinds. It's been an incredible privilege to do this work.

Thanks to Rebecca Katz, Carina Chacon, and the rest of the team at New Deal Strategies for guiding our communications throughout 2024, and to Stephanie Schriock for your unflinching advice and mentorship.

To all the friends and group-chat combinations who've been both excellent pals and thought partners—in no particular order, I'm forever grateful to Amy Biehl, Taylor Salditch, Liz Zaretsky, Nichole Sessego, Danielle Kantor, Kate Stayman-London, Jess Morales Rocketto, Jenna Lowenstein, Danielle Butterfield, Patrick Stevenson, Julie Zuckerbrod, Alex Wall, Caitlin Mitchell, Ezra Mechaber, KP Trueblood, Ashley Bernick, Kirsten Koretz, Maddie Boardman, and Scott Ritter.

Thanks to my therapist, Dr. Jacob Kaplan, who continually reminded me throughout that year that I had said in December that 2024 was going to be very hard—and at the very least, it's satisfying to be right.

I don't have the time or energy to survive without full-time childcare during the week—so thank you to the incredible caregivers at our daughters' day care who, if there was any justice in the world, would each be millionaires.

Thanks to my parents for being fully unimpressed when I said I was writing a new book—it's important to stay humble—and to my siblings, Jessi, Daniel, and Vicky, for being my first followers. And she'll never read this, because she's a dog, but thanks to Sadie for being my constant companion through two whole books.

Finally, to my family.

My husband, Declan, who has been a better and more loving partner than I ever could have imagined for myself. Thank you for believing in me when I said sometime during the summer of 2023, "Resolved: I'm going to write another book," and then giving me the time, space, and support to do it—even when it meant lots of solo parenting our mischievous toddler. I am so lucky to be the recipient of your endless patience, your steady presence, and your measured perspective. You make even the worst days if not exactly fun then at least eventually pretty funny in retrospect. I love our life together.

And our daughters: My big girl Jo, whose first year of life kicked all this off, and baby Franny, who grew inside me each week along with my word count. I hope the only cycle you feel the need to break is my complete inability to decide what to eat for dinner. Love you both to the moon.

NOTES

Introduction

1. "Red, White, and Gray," *Business Insider*, September 13, 2022, www.businessinsider.com/gerontocracy-united-states-government-red-white-gray-2022-9.
2. Ben Lindbergh and Rob Arthur, "The Golden Age of the Aging Actor," *The Ringer*, July 27, 2022, www.theringer.com/movies/2022/6/27/23181232/old-actors-aging-tom-cruise-top-gun-maverick.
3. Paul Millerd, "The Boomer Blockade: How One Generation Shaped the Workforce and Left Everyone Behind," January 24, 2020, pmillerd.com/the-boomer-blockade.
4. Derek Thompson, "Why the Old Elite Spend So Much Time at Work," *The Atlantic*, August 3, 2022, www.theatlantic.com/newsletters/archive/2022/08/older-aging-politicians-athletes-culture/671027.
5. Marc Fischer, "Older Americans Are Dominating Like Never Before, but What Comes Next?" *The Washington Post*, October 24, 2023, https://news.yahoo.com/older-americans-dominating-never-comes-192112325.html.
6. Nick Lichtenberg, "Millennials are Officially the Majority of Managers–So Get Ready for a Combination of Burnout, Buddy Vibes, and Boundary Issues," *Fortune*, July 23, 2025, https://fortune.com/2025/07/23/millennial-managers-burnout-cool-boss-boundary-issues-glassdoor-worklife-trends-daniel-zhao/

How to Be Yourself (But Responsibly)

1. Sylvia Ann Hewlett, *Executive Presence 2.0: Leadership in an Age of Inclusion* (HarperCollins, 2023).
2. Adam Grant, "Unless You're Oprah, 'Be Yourself' Is Terrible Advice," *The New York Times*, June 4, 2016, www.nytimes.com/2016/06/05/opinion/sunday/unless-youre-oprah-be-yourself-is-terrible-advice.html.
3. Analiza Quiroz Wolf, *The Myths of Success: A Woman of Color's Guide to Leadership* (Wishful Wolf Press, 2024).
4. Rachel Wilkerson Miller, *The Art of Showing Up: How to Be There for Yourself and Your People* (The Experiment, 2020).

Redefining Professionalism

1. Anne Helen Petersen, "A Theory of the Modern Exclamation Point!: Doing the Work of Tone," *Culture Study*, January 7, 2024, annehelen.substack.com/p/a-theory-of-the-modern-exclamation.

What Happens on the Internet Rarely Stays on the Internet

1. Rachel Kowert and Emory Daniel Jr., "The One-and-a-Half Sided Parasocial Relationship: The Curious Case of Live Streaming," *Computers in Human Behavior Reports* 4 (August–December 2021), www.sciencedirect.com/science/article/pii/S2451958821000981.

People Should Be Their Real Selves, Not Their Full Selves

1. Derek Thompson, "Workism Is Making Americans Miserable," *The Atlantic*, February 24, 2019, www.theatlantic.com/ideas/archive/2019/02/religion-workism-making-americans-miserable/583441.
2. Kelly Main and Rob Watts, "Workplace Romance Statistics: Survey Shows Employees Engage Regularly in Office Relationships," *Forbes*, April 30, 2024, 10:13 p.m., www.forbes.com/advisor/business/workplace-romance-statistics.
3. Neta Achdut and Tehila Refaeli, "Unemployment and Psychological Distress among Young People during the COVID-19 Pandemic: Psychological Resources and Risk Factors," *International Journal of Environmental Research and Public Health* 17, no. 19 (October 2020), www.ncbi.nlm.nih.gov/pmc/articles/PMC7579061.

4. *The R.O.I. of Caregiving Benefits* (Vivvi and Fifth Trimester, 2023), go.vivvi.com/the-roi-of-caregiving-benefits-vivvi-the-fifth-trimester.
5. Katie Merritt, "Remote work statistics and trends for 2026," roberthalf.com, April 23, 2026, https://www.roberthalf.com/us/en/insights/research/remote-work-statistics-and-trends
6. Marc Shorb, "Essential Return-To-Office Statistics and Trends," Founder Reports, November 10, 2025, https://founderreports.com/return-to-office-statistics/

In Order to Work Better, You Need to Rest Better

1. 4 Day Week Global / Boston College, published Nature Human Behaviour, July 2025. Cited by The Interview Guys, 'Four-Day Workweek Goes Global,' Oct 2025 , https://blog.theinterviewguys.com/four-day-workweek-goes-global/, https://www.apollotechnical.com/four-day-work-week-statistics/
2. Matt Egan, "4-Day Workweeks May Be Around the Corner. A Third of America's Companies Are Exploring Them," CNN, April 12, 2024, 10:54 a.m. EDT, www.cnn.com/2024/04/12/business/four-day-workweek-survey/index.html

Transparency: Can You Be Too Honest?

1. Joseph Grenny, Kerry Patterson, Ron McMillan, Al Switzler, and Emily Gregory, *Crucial Conversations: Tools for Talking When Stakes Are High*, 3rd ed. (McGraw Hill, 2021). Much of this was taken from *Crucial Conversations*, although it was influenced by other management and leadership trainings over the years. These are not new!
2. Grenny et al., *Crucial Conversations*, 26.
3. Jedediah Britton-Purdy, "We've Been Thinking About America's Trust Collapse All Wrong," *The Atlantic*, January 8, 2024, www.theatlantic.com/ideas/archive/2024/01/trust-democracy-liberal-government/677035.
4. Jordan Lippert and Jonathan Schulman, "Where Most People Trust Others and Where They Don't Around the World," Pew Research Center, December 1, 2025, https://www.pewresearch.org/short-reads/2025/12/01/where-most-people-trust-others-and-where-they-dont-around-the-world/

How We Survive: Finding Community and Joy

1. Soraya Chemaly, *The Resilience Myth: New Thinking on Grit, Strength, and Growth After Trauma* (Simon & Schuster, 2024), 205.

We Do Not Dream of Labor

1. Malcolm Harris, *Kids These Days: Human Capital and the Making of Millennials* (Little, Brown, 2017).
2. Elizabeth Faber, "2025 Gen Z and Millennial Survey: Growth and the Pursuit of Money, Meaning, and Well-Being," Deloitte, 2025, https://deloitte.com/global/en/issues/work/genz-millennial-survey.html

ABOUT THE AUTHOR

AMANDA LITMAN is the cofounder and president of Run for Something, which recruits and supports young, diverse leaders running for local office. Since 2017, they've launched the careers of thousands of millennials and Gen Z candidates and, in the process, changed what leadership looks like in America. She's also the author of *Run for Something: A Real-Talk Guide to Fixing the System Yourself*, a how-to manual for people running for office.

Before launching Run for Something, Amanda worked on multiple presidential and statewide political campaigns. She graduated from Northwestern University and lives in Brooklyn with her husband, two daughters, and their sometimes rowdy dog.